MW01244492

AMELIA EARHART, ME & OUR FRIENDS

Journaling the Journey

The Amelia Earhart Self Help Book

BY

ROBERTA ELLEN BASSIN

FOREWORD BY ELGEN M. LONG
AUTHOR OF
"AMELIA EARHART,
THE MYSTERY SOLVED"

© June 15, 2015 • Febrary, 2016 • Jaunuary, 2017 • June, 2020
ISBN-13: 978-1523738564
ISBN-10: 1523738561

Design, Graphics and Layout
Sigrid K. Powell

Author: Roberta Ellen Bassin
www.RobertaBassin.com

DEDICATION
of My Play and Book

To My Husband,

Who patiently produced, schlepped, built sets,
listened over and over again, introduced, publicized,
created brochures, stage managed,
encouraged, supported, took me to lunch,
drove, carried--all outside his engineering-
private-person, non-theatrical,
comfort zone--and glowed with pride and love
at every one of our productions.

I love you and thank you, my Neddel.

Amelia Earhart, Me & Our Friends

Journaling the Journey

CONTENTS

ACKNOWLEDGEMENTS

My heartfelt appreciation to all those who have supported me in numerous ways as I navigated the uncharted waters of developing and performing my play "Amelia Earhart: In Her Own Words," which has led to the writing and publication of "Amelia Earhart, Me and Our Friends: Journaling the Journey. The Amelia Earhart Self Help Book."

You know who you are, but the world needs to know. And so with pride, smiles and applause, I give a standing ovation to all of you: those I've known a lifetime and those I've met along the way.

First and foremost to my family. My over-the-top supportive husband, Ned Franklin Bassin, to whom I dedicated my play and book, who for years has heard me rehearsing, was patient as I wrote, read and reread my book, went running to different venues, and all that goes with being a performer and writer. Your patience, love and understanding are beyond measure.

To my son, Daryl Evan Bassin, who I trusted to be the first person to read my book in its entirety. He not only was my first editor but also gave me constant encouragement and support to keep me going forward with the process. My heart swells with pride that we are not only mother and son but also best of friends.

To my daughter, Corinne Juliet Bassin, whose strength of determination and responsibility along with the beautiful family she has created, give me joy and fortitude.

To my mother Sally Kaufman and my aunt Lillian Cope, whose love, support and dedication to my upbringing and life were unsurpassed.

To my talented writing friends, whose interest, knowledge and research on the most famous of females aviators, Amelia Mary Earhart, supported both me as artist of stage, screen and television and now in my newest endeavor as author of this book.

To Giacinta Bradley Koontz, author, lecturer, aviation historian, whom I met when she attended one of my early performances becoming a friend, mentor and motivational supporter of all my endeavors. She kept me going to get this book completed. Her generous contribution of photos from her private collection, as well as her extensive knowledge and experience as an author of books (The Harriet Quimby Scrapbook, Pioneer Mechanics and The Original Grand Canyon Airport) and articles, was truly a prized gift.

To Elgen M. Long and Kay Long, one of the most fun and inspirational couples I know, sharing, supporting and motivating me whenever I reached out to them. I thank Elgen for the lovely Foreword for "Amelia Earhart, Me and Our Friends." He continues to research Amelia in a follow up edition to his book, entitled "Amelia Earhart, The Mystery Solved." He also continues to write books on his flying experiences, including the airlifts of Yemenite Jews to Palestine. Elgen generously gave me numerous photographs from his private collection of and relating to Amelia Earhart, for which I am deeply grateful.

To actress, author and radio hostess, Debbie Zipp, who was my first advisor. She gave me invaluable guidelines and encouragement as I was about to initiate the writing of my book. I was very honored when she and her writing partner, Molly Cheek, invited me to be a contributor to their wonderful book, "The Aspiring Actor's Handbook: What Seasoned Actors Wished They Had Known."

To Emily Lodmer, my lifelong friend since our graduation from UCLA, who read my first and additional manuscripts editing along the way in minute detail, never shying away from a challenge. She has been there for me in thick and thin and attended my performances many times . . . repeatedly . . . that's friendship.

To Daniel Kessler, who with joyful volition, amazing sharpness of eye and extraordinary knowledge of punctuation and grammar, was a diligent proofreader.

To Sigrid (Siggy) Powell, who patiently encouraged, and did the final editing and formatting for this first-time book author. She continues to add her magic book polish. Thank you for making my manuscript into a truly beautiful book, of which we can be proud.

To all those new friends, organizations and Amelia Earhart enthusiasts who have also enriched my life and led me to creating "Amelia Earhart, Me and Our Friends." My apologies to any I have inadvertently left out. Here are but a few in alphabetical order: Laura Schaffer Bozoukoff, the late Gabriel Bresnik, Randy Bresnik, Molly Murphy MacGregor, Tuskegee Airman Victor Miller, the late George Palmer Putnum Jr., and Marie Putnam, Ann Pellegreno, Fred Tonsing, John Underwood, Dan Witkoff. Organizations: The Loni Chapman Group Repertory Company, Women in Theatre, National Women's History Project, Santa Monica Museum of Flying, The 99s, The Amelia Earhart Library, Boeing, Raytheon, Cradle of Aviation, Embry-Riddle University.

I feel so very lucky and blessed to have you all and the countless wonderful friends, extended family and fans who have been there, encouraged me and brighten my world every single day. With heartfelt appreciation, I thank you.

x

FOREWORD

by Elgen M. Long

Written October 14, 2014

"You bring Amelia Earhart to life." That was my reaction when I first saw Roberta Bassin performing her one woman show, Amelia Earhart: In Her Own Words. It was for a breakfast honoring George Palmer Putnam Jr., Amelia's stepson and youngest son of the famous publisher George Palmer Putnam.

Since then, our friendship and connection grew from our mutual interest in the most famous female aviator of all time. Our passion for historical veracity and enthusiasm for learning is a joy we both share and admire. Amelia brought us and so many interested friends together.

As an aviator, adventurer, writer and family man, I know the drive that takes hold of one to accomplish goals for which we hunger. It had been suggested to Roberta, many times, that with the extent of her knowledge and research on Amelia Earhart, a book was a logical step. But, as she said at one of her performances, "There are enough books about Amelia Earhart."

However, as more and more fans clamored for a publication based on so many years of research, performances, and changing perspectives, Roberta finally acquiesced. Nevertheless, she wanted to write a book that was atypical of the usual books about Amelia.

Amelia had become a strong connection in Roberta's life since she wrote the full-length play many years ago, staying on top of all current news, theories and legacy that are Earhart. Roberta's perspective of Amelia would change as her own life changed, answering many of life's questions for herself and her audiences.

It occurred to Roberta that this was what had been most helpful to her. It was what she had learned from Amelia's words. This could be helpful to others also, she surmised. Thus Amelia Earhart, Me and Our Friends – Journaling the Journey was born.

Elgen M. Long
http://elgenlong.com/

First solo flight around-the-world over both Poles.

Author: *Amelia Earhart: The Mystery Solved* the book by Elgen M. Long and Mary Long detailing 35 years of research into the Crash and Sank theory.

Consultant on the 2009 feature film, "Amelia" starring Hilary Swank and Richard Gere, directed by Mira Nair, written by Ronald Bass.

INTRODUCTION
Face the Wind

Hello, I am Amelia Mary Earhart! In actuality, I am Roberta Ellen Bassin, actress and writer. I perform as the great aviatrix in my one-woman show, *Amelia Earhart: In Her Own Words.*

Amelia and I have developed a relationship through my play. How did our connection, our unique relationship of over twenty-five years ever happen? I am as puzzled as anyone, and pleasantly surprised to think that I came to inhabit the character of Amelia Earhart in the simplest of ways.

I was a member of a repertory company. The theatre director had posted a list of historical characters from which the members were to choose. Then we were to write a play about that character. For no particular reason that I could put my finger on at the time, I chose Amelia Earhart. As with choosing anything in life: career, mate, clothes, something about her just appealed to me. All these years later, my interest has not waned.

As actor and author, performing my one-woman play for many years, I have been continually researching Amelia Earhart's history. My perspectives are always changing. I see Amelia's words differently as my own life experiences change, but I always take comfort in the lessons Amelia Earhart's life and writings offer. One day it occurred to me, if her words are so motivating and helpful to *me*, then it should follow that I could motivate and inspire others by sharing our journey – Amelia's and mine – and now you can also share yours by means of this journal.

This is probably the first "adults only," amusing, interactive Amelia Earhart self help book ever written. Writing this book has turned out to be a more enjoyable exploration, taking me to a new realm beyond the performance aspect, than I ever expected. As Amelia said (and was highly criticized for by the press), "To me fun is the indispensable part of work!" Writing about Amelia Earhart has certainly been fun – in addition to being insightful – for me.

This book, *Amelia Earhart, Me and Our Friends*, is the story of my journey as a performer telling Amelia Earhart's story and my changing perspectives, connection and relationship with her. Learning about this remarkable woman and relating to her, I learn about myself. I see how we are alike and dissimilar – and have come to understand the reasons for our similarities and differences. As in any journal, there are entry dates. However, I have organized the entries topically. Thus, they are not consecutive. I hope you approve.

Meet *Amelia, Me and Our Friends*. Enjoy our paths, one large and well known, the other small and less famous, intersecting and touching. This is our story: the presenter and the heroine on an unexpected journey, and now you are invited to join us.

A retrospective letter to the great aviator:

> Dear Amelia,
> I see your influence. It is as strong as ever. You and I can motivate others by telling your story. I am merely the vehicle. The need for an example like yours is as current for women today as it was in the past. The mystery of your disappearance keeps you, ironically, alive throughout the world.
>
> Secretary of State Hillary Clinton stated in 2012:
> *She (Amelia Earhart) gave people hope and she inspired them to dream bigger and bolder. When she took off on that historic journey, she carried the aspirations of our entire country with her . . . We too could use some of Amelia's spirit, that sense that anything is possible if we just roll up our sleeves and get to work together.*[1]
>
> I've met those who knew you, Amelia, such as your competitor, Bobby Trout, your stepson, George Palmer Putnam, Jr. and other men and women – both famous and not so famous – including family members and critics.

Mechanics, observers, farmers and fliers, students and teachers, writers and readers all gain hope, vision and strength from your story and your unexpected adventure.

Your faults, frailties, talents, remoteness, public and private coping mechanisms and drive, your humanness and your unique persona never cease to fascinate. They allow us, your observers, to identify and see our own selves.

Your passion allows us to identify our own passions. Your courage reminds us to be courageous, to go after what we want, be who we are – and that itself will reap the greatest benefits for all. Your goal setting and sense of optimism, adventure, performing feats only attempted by a handful, many unsung heroes and heroines, have paved the way for the rest of us to fashion our own path and sing our own song out loud.

Sincerely,
Roberta

As at the beginning of my one-woman show and now at the beginning of this book, I greet you, our reader, with a warm welcome.

Amelia and I are unexpected and unlikely partners. Our paths, friendships and public interactions have been – and continue to be – a fabulous, adventurous journey. Our stories, what Amelia said about various issues, how I see her point of view, Amelia's pictures, mine, her friends and mine, all intersect in new and surprising ways.

As a result of these intersections, I have recognized new perspectives related to my life experiences, in addition to new ways to view and cope with them.

There is no end to gaining new observations/assessments as one gains experience and age. From my theatrical bent, I see these events analogous to the curtain that draws down on the last show or stage of life experience, only to rise up for an encore presenting new horizons, new people, places and points of view.

To My Readers,

If I repeat tales of certain life events, it is only because life and one's own patterns repeat themselves, teaching multiple lessons in the process.

I see repetition as growth (a sort of spiraling), and I hope you will indulge me and yourselves in seeing the repetition, ebb and flow of your own behavior and thoughts in a positive light.

Throughout my study of Ms. Earhart, my audiences and I have been curious about her thought patterns and perspectives. Thus, you will see questions posed for thoughtful discussion to probe into Amelia's mindset and your own.

For example: Did Amelia Earhart relax, contemplate, allow creativity to flow and formulate into a multitude of worthy ideas? An individual can consider such questions for him or herself. I feel I've gotten to know Amelia's mind much deeper and closer by pondering such questions. That feels good as an actor understanding a character, as a writer delving into a story, as a student learning. It is deliciously fun, exhilarating and yes, relaxing.

And now we (Amelia and I) are asking you to join us, as our friends, on your own new adventure to learn more about yourself, gain answers and discover personal insights. I hope you write repeatedly too. Perhaps journal your own journey along with Amelia Earhart and me. Enjoy yourselves. "Ready for take off?" Let's GOOOOO Explore!

CHAPTER ONE

WE WRITE, RIGHT.

MOTIVATING OTHERS: AMELIA, WRITER FRIEND, ME

Written December 18, 2011

The other night at a holiday party, a writer friend said three little words, "Write every day." Somehow, this resonated with me at that moment. After a week spent floating in the recesses of my mind, I woke up one morning positively motivated in life and forward-looking in career and writing.

Molly Murphy MacGregor, co-founder of the National Women's History Project, reminded me that motivating others by performing as Amelia Earhart does change people. If it changes even one person's life, it can change the world in unforeseen ways, to hope for the better.

Dear Reader . . .

Have you either been motivated or motivated others by some small or large action?

Enjoy jotting a few of these thoughts down as we jounal our journey of self-awareness together.

TITLE IDEA: AMELIA EARHART'S SELF HELP BOOK

Written July 22, 2013

I had just written in my personal journal about being overwhelmed. I connected this emotion to the formulation of a question about Amelia for my Amelia Earhart book in development. I realized that I was writing out my confusion in order to help myself through assessing my knowledge of Amelia, figuring out how best to connect with my audience, – you – and asking, "Did Amelia experience similar thoughts, dilemmas, events?"

Light bulb effect! Excitement! Explosive realization!!!! This is a self-help book, not just for me, but for my readers.

I see that the topical discussions I write about affect everyone. My idea is to show that Amelia, whether famous or not, was just like the rest of us dealing with personal issues, getting through the day, whether good, bad or just pain ordinary. How Amelia dealt with her personal and public life has been a fascinating, enriching and helpful education for me, and I whole-heartedly believe it will be for you as well.

She found herself on the world stage, a platform from which to voice her views. Today anyone can make his or her own platform on the internet via blogging, Facebook and other social media.

Amelia was headstrong, diplomatically outspoken, multitasking, family oriented, independent, athletic and a "daredevil tomboy" before becoming "Lady Lindy" as described by the newspapers.

Thus, Amelia was – and still is – teaching us. We can learn from "the girl who walked alone," a quotation from her yearbook.[1]

Join me on our expedition through the mind, adventures and everyday ups and downs of the mysterious, lively, creative woman, who designed her own clothes, wrote poetry, enjoyed photography and gardening.

Who also embraced the roles of family provider, sports woman and model, yet was controlling, independent, shy and determined.

Amelia was a woman of opposites. Her appearance was androgynous yet feminine. She was fascinating and attractive to men, yet unthreatening to women, mechanic of cars and planes, writer and first president of the 99s, the first all female aviators organization.

Now it is your turn. I invite you to make your own self-descriptive list.

If you aren't aware of it already, you are a fascinating, multitalented, multitasking, interesting, knowledgeable, admirable person who, if interviewed, would fascinate any reader or listener. Start with the obvious. Start writing, and you too will find and surprise yourself.

This realization helped and continues to help me. I hope it will be helpful, interesting, fun and enlightening for you, my friends and readers, too.

ENJOY and follow your Passions.

Dear Reader . . .

It is your turn, if you like, to share your own self-descriptive list.

You may even surprise yourself!

Enjoy.

9/11 JOURNALING: A CATHARTIC JOURNEY

Written September 10, 2011 9:02 a.m.

Anniversary of 9/11. Look where flight has taken its toll. Amelia predicted flight would be "as commonplace as train travel." Amelia had become fascinated with airplanes when living in Toronto, Canada.

> I believe it was during the winter of 1918 that I became interested in airplanes. Though I had seen one or two at county fairs before, I now saw many of them, as the officers were trained at the various fields around the city. Of course, no civilian had the opportunity of going up. But I hung around in my spare time and absorbed all I could. I remember the sting of the snow on my face as it was blown back from the propellers when the training planes took off on skis. I remember well when that snow stung my face I felt the first urge to fly.[2]

So, Amelia became interested in flight and the mechanics of the plane itself, during a time of war, which advanced its technology too. I guess, there will always be armed conflict and whatever tools are available to the warriors will be employed to their advantage.

I was afraid to face dealing with or even writing today's date. But this, as all writing, has been freeing, cathartic and clarifying. Maybe and of course, it must have been the same for Amelia. She wrote much poetry, newsletters, magazine articles, and always journaling. Boxes of personal letters were found in her Mother's last apartment in Berkley, California.

REVISITED, NEED TO WRITE, CAN'T REMEMBER

Did Amelia Have Trouble Remembering?
Written September 18, 2013

Amelia probably had many thoughts, fleeting thoughts she wanted to put in her books, personal letters, poems, 99s newsletters, the press, which if not jotted down immediately would be forgotten. Wow, she had been doing much writing, so that must have happened . . . many times.

I know she jotted down her thoughts in sometimes difficult-to-read notes and sent them back to George Palmer Putnam on her round-the-world flight. GP had a book planned for every major flight. He was her promoter and husband who had their best financial interest at hand.

My disappearing thought of *Amelia and Me* occurred while I was driving my car. I couldn't or didn't want to pull over "just to jot it down," certain I would remember it when I got home.

Well, it has been 24 hours, and "no dice." I am still searching for it in my mind. I feel it floating around. Even as I write this entry, hoping it will percolate to the surface, form a full thought and travel out my mouth translated into the written word . . . let's hope.

Meanwhile, it now occurs to me that even though everyone attributes George Putnam pushing Amelia to write books of her flights, she was always a natural writer, having submitted poems under the name Emile A. Hart.

Even as a child, she wrote with flair and her personality filtered through.

Amelia, 1903

10

(Letter) 4th Birthday

    DEAR GRANDMA, I GOT A STOVE WITH A
        TEA KETTLE AND PAN. A DOLL AND
        SOME BOOKS.
        I LOVE YOU AND THANK YOU.
           YOUR LOVING MILLIE.[3]

Amelia always kept a journal on her flights. Did she keep a personal diary? Voila! Her words in my play, Amelia's quotation, "I remember thinking and jotting down . . . when I was a small girl in Atchison Kansas."[4] There is the answer. She was always "jotting down." People who like to write, which usually transfers to "need to write," probably keep notes more naturally than non-writers.

Amelia was a very private, savvy individual and smart about the press. She most likely would have not put on paper anything that might be misconstrued, taken the wrong way or be self-incriminating.

In the same vain, there are glimpses of her warnings to her mother on airing unpopular political views. In one of her letters advising her mother, she writes, "Don't talk about your socialist leanings . . . or criticize the Roosevelts . . . the most popular people on the planet," with whom Amelia was personal friends.[5]

Amelia and her mother, Amy Otis Earhart.

Whew, I feel much better after writing a bit. Does this mean that when I finish this book, if I ever do, I will need to keep writing? If that is true, then to feel pressure that this will never be accomplished and if it is then I'm finished, is an illogical conclusion.

Somehow this is comforting, because I am always feeling I have to hurriedly finish whatever I am doing, "never staying long enough to enjoy where I am" as Amelia put it when circumnavigating the globe on her last flight. As she added, "I have a schedule, I must abide by it, this is not a voyage of sight seeing. Oh but there are so many sights I wanted to see."[6]

So we are similar in many ways, or maybe this is human nature. The irony of enjoying the moment, but to accomplish a goal, one must maintain a schedule.

Amelia, our heroine, was a real person who struggled with all the issues we struggle with: big and small, family, business, financial, artistic, everyday life and momentous events. One can compare notes and learn, identify and commiserate as human beings trying to make it all work out to the best of our ability, developing whatever we've got, to go for "the stars."

Follow your dreams, passions, and visions. Remember, Amelia Earhart had a bad back, severe sinus condition and a weak stomach. She was physically ill suited for long distance flying, but her desire to fly consumed her to greatness.

ACCIDENTS HAPPEN

Written December 27, 2011

I had my plans. A simple day. I had made a play date for exercise, lunch and the usual girl chitchat.

As I was about to leave, the phone rings. "What are you doing right now?" says a calm sweet voice without pressure. It is my son. It turns out his car had sputtered and thumped in a loud rhythm. He was at a mechanics shop and was hopeful I could pick him up. "Of course. I'm there for you."

I called my friend, explaining the situation. The best-made plans sometimes must be changed. Amelia was no exception.

Amelia was always waiting for or adapting to weather changes, alcoholic drunken pilots, and the most difficult, the crash on takeoff of the Lockheed Electra on Amelia's first attempt to fly around the world on March 20, 1937.

This was the first time Amelia felt fear, "I don't know what happened." Two minutes later she emerged from the cockpit, "I knew what I wanted to do. If we don't burn up I want to try again."[7]

And she did "try again." On May 20, 1937, she and her husband (George Palmer Putnam, also known as GP or GPP) with an $80,000 donation from Purdue University rebuilt the Lockheed Electra. GP had to reschedule all the refueling contracts and locations. The entire trip had to be revamped, now going eastward, adding two thousand more miles of flight distance from 27,000 miles to 29,000.

Weather conditions would be more difficult, and still worse, Amelia's team including technical advisor, Paul Mantz, and expert radioman Harry Manning would no longer be able to continue. GP, her husband, was left to do all the planning, technical and otherwise, (which he had not done before) along with Fred Noonan, PAN AM navigator, the best in the business, but lacked knowledge of radio technology.

13

Mishaps can change things for better or worse. Would Amelia have made it if all elements remained the same after her initial try, we'll never know.

DEFEAT AND MOTIVATION

Written July 30, 2013

Did Amelia ever feel defeated, lose motivation, feel overwhelmed by others' seemingly successful "BS"?

I went to a networking birthday party last night. Instead of feeling joyful and fun filled, it left me this morning with next day blues. Being bombarded by others' career spin, "fake it till you make it," whether fabricated or just excellent creative self-promotion, left me feeling stuck and unmotivated.

I knew intellectually, it depends on one's definition of success. For me, it is a completion of tasks, going for the gold, never giving up, following one's dreams and passions.

Looking back, I felt like I wasn't gaining ground, when in fact, I had made steady progress. One way or another, I have kept my hat in the ring.

Accomplishing small goals each day is a good way to feel positive about yourself. Moving forward just makes me smile, like just now when I stepped on the scale and saw I lost a couple of ounces (that I wanted to lose).

I also find that writing down each morning three successes from the day before, however small, and five gratefuls for which I am blessed, starts my day in a positive light. For example: yesterday I practiced my vocal exercises, ate oatmeal with blueberries, went to a networking event and when I was feeling rejected, employed a mantra "embrace everyone regardless of their position," which my career coach Dallas Travers and I developed from taking her class. It worked, and I overcame the barrier of discomfort between me and folks I deemed more successful than me.

I am grateful for my wonderful husband who loves me, is there for me and listens to all my ups and downs. I am grateful for my children, my family, my longtime friends and even acquaintances who I can talk with, be silly with or just ask to "come out and play" as we used to say as children.

Try making a list of your successes and gratefuls. You'll be glad you did. Me too.

Do I think Amelia ever felt defeated, overwhelmed? Probably. I noticed from her letters that celebrity made her feel overwhelmed. That she became more private with more success, more guarded around the press and public. But feeling defeated, it is difficult to determine.

Of course, during her ultimate demise, as she radioed that she was out of fuel in her last few minutes of flight before disappearing over the Pacific, her voice was shrill over the radio trying to communicate with the ship, Itasca.

It was 8:44 a.m. "We are on the line of position 156-137/. Will repeat message. We will repeat message pm 6210K. Listening on 6210K. We are running North and South."[8]

Itasca responded transmitting by voice and key. No answer.

And then nothing.

Was this defeat, fear, desperation for survival? Most likely and then did she land on an atoll still hopeful to be rescued, never giving up? Somehow my emotions hope for that.

Dear Reader . . .

Congratulate yourself, acknowledging your successes and all for which you are grateful each day, no matter how small.

Feel your smile radiate from inside out. Your shinning light will reflect back from others, creating more joy.

Here's your happy space:

Jot down three successes and five gratefuls.

Successes and Greatfuls:

CHAPTER TWO
FASHION, FUN & PHYSICAL APPEARANCE

PARTIES, PARTIES, PARTIES

Written May 28, 2013

I've never had so many family, friend, and Emmy Award time parties and events. I want to be included, liked, loved – and even if I don't really want to attend – I want to be invited. Geez!

As soon as Amelia Earhart crossed the Atlantic in 1928 as a passenger and landed in Burry Port, Wales, the parties were never-ending. Accepting awards, dancing with the Prince of Wales, tea with Lady Astor, days with dignitaries, accepting awards.

I am always exhausted, drained, needing R&R after each event. Yet, I finish one and find myself looking for the next, not wanting to be left out, not wanting to miss anything, thinking about what I will wear, creating outfits much the same as Amelia, who also enjoyed fashion design. "It was like the bells to the fire horse, I was right there snorting," as Amelia put it.[1]

Like me, Amelia was basically a private person, naturally inclined to shy away from media, fans and the limelight, but also motivated to seek challenges which involved being in that very high profile life. Totally a world of contrasts, personally conflicting and yet tantalizingly tempting. Truly a personality mystery of sorts. Perhaps we all have them.

Maybe the attraction to be a guest of such events has as much to do with being included as it does with creating fashion, "playing dress up" for both Amelia and me. Since childhood, Amelia had always created or redesigned her and Muriel's clothes.

I know that part of my enjoyment in being an actor comes from creating costumes for each audition, show, event and, yes, party. I found voiceover work less attractive than stage acting in large part because voiceover actors show up in sweats – costumes not required. Not for me! Funny, isn't it?

Dear Reader . . .

Consider: Why did Amelia do the social circuit?

How about You?

Do you attend events you feel uncomfortable about whether for business, family or other obligations?

What is the upside of attending such events for you?

My style: The plane adds a special touch, don't you think?

Dear Reader . . .

What is your personal style, preference "My rules, My style?"

Enjoy or find a photo of your true self-style. We all have one.

AMELIA AND HER WEIGHT

Written August 25, 2013

(On this day August 25, 1932: Amelia Earhart becomes the first woman to fly nonstop across the United States, traveling from Los Angeles to Newark, New Jersey, in 19 hours.)

Did Amelia ever worry about her weight?

I saw myself in a filmed audition. I was surprised to see a pronounced tummy! I knew that after we came home from our friend's daughter's wedding, finding the refrigerator out of commission, and being sooo hungry, I ate all combinations of food and larger meals than usual. BAM! The couple of pounds came on, and I went from looking slim to a little chubby. Amazing!

I don't think Amelia ever had that happen. If anything, it looks like the reverse. "No time for luncheon" was her statement when GP called and said, "good flying weather, fine visibility all the way" regarding an opening to take off for her solo Atlantic flight.[2]

Food was not a priority for Amelia.

On her round-the-world flight, getting only five hours of sleep a night, always having a weak stomach and back, Amelia looks emaciated, almost skeleton like, in her last photos.

In her normal everyday life, she was always model-like and she did do modeling in 1934 of her clothing line.

HER HANDS, MY HANDS

Written September 2011

As I rehearsed my play for yet another gig, it occurred to me how similar our hands were. "Piano fingers" my mother used to say, which she noticed when I was born.

Amelia had "piano fingers" also. Looking at her photographs, especially where her fingers are spread over the world globe, shows their smooth, graceful beauty. This was surprising, since she did many sports, gardening, flying and actually working on the engine of her car. You see their loveliness when she holds the steer [sic] wheel of the Lockheed Electra.[3]

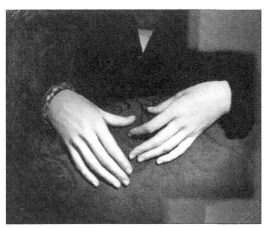 

"The tapering loveliness of her hands was almost unbelievable, found in one who did the things she did," wrote George Putnam in his biography of Amelia Earhart in "Soaring Wings."

It seems logical that she took good care of her hands. She did care about her appearance, always carrying a compact to powder her nose before exiting the plane when reporters might appear, and lipstick too.

Amelia also was concerned about her mother's presentation and appearance. For example, she gave extensive instructions to her mother on proper attire for her European cruise, in the following letter:

> Suggest you wear dark blue wool for departure and landing if not too warm. It looks so swell.
> Keep manicured and have hair done every 10 days.
> Use Vince after every meal more often if not feeling well. Important.
> If raining don't wear kid gloves. They'll spot and be ruined. Wear washables or fabric.
> I have given you very decent stockings . . . If lying down with knees bent loosen garters to decrease pull over knees. Do not yank any hose on from top.
>
> Evening dresses
> Most formal gray lace with blue jacket
> Next blue net with white fur jacket
> Next, transformed blue nightgown
> This last is just a dinner dress
> Save the gray for the festive night on the boat. There always is one.
> Last, Have a good time.[4]

This is a favorite letter of mine. It tells us so much about Amelia. Take what you will from this letter but Amelia was apparently fastidious about appearance, every minute detail, and it was important to her that those connected to her would present a positive image.

Whether Amelia took up the piano, I have no evidence. I myself have made some attempt, but "piano fingers," as many genetic gifts, do not guarantee there is talent or that it will be developed and used.

I marvel, as George Putnam did, at Amelia's absolutely smooth, graceful hands, as seen in these photos.

LIVING THE DREAM:
THE ULTIMATE HIGH AND FASHION TOO!

Written February 21, 2012 9:36am

"If there is anything I have learned in life it is this: If you follow the inner desire of your heart, the incidentals will take care of themselves." —Amelia Earhart.

Last night I performed three staged readings at a little playhouse, under the banner "Love: Lost and Found." All three characters we're different, interesting and looking for love. I had to create unique quick changes and efficient costuming because the stories were about ten minutes apart. I loved creating clever ways of doing this all with a basic dress and different accessories.

Amelia, as mentioned, also loved creating and designing clothes as with her first flight suit, greasing up her leather jacket to look like the other fliers. "You know women pilots had a lot of trouble getting practical clothes to wear flying. We had to buy men's clothes," commented Amelia.

Due to Amelia's lengthy body structure, arms and waistlines were always too short; redesigning was almost a necessity. In my case, I was always trying to avoid the sun due to my fair skin. This was before sunscreen lotions, when summer clothing was always based on skimpiness. For me, clothing had to be lightweight, cool, stylish and protective from the sun's burning rays. I enjoyed sewing, creating, making my own clothes, and eventually bedspreads, cloth toys, and other items of stitching and cloth.

Similarly, my clothing had to have "ease of movement and simplicity" too.

"Fame works in mysterious ways. I was criticized for cropping my hair and wearing pants, when in 1934 I found myself designing fashion, modeling and writing for fashion magazines." So Amelia Earhart became a fashion designer.[5]

Now how did I get sidetracked from pursuing one's dream to designing? Ah yes! The designing was part of the enjoyment of developing and enjoying my, and as noted, Amelia's dream. It was and is part of the whole.

Her flying must have given her the "high" (pun unintentional but appropriate) of success. That "fix" of accomplishment makes one continue to pursue, enjoy, learn, improve, promote, educate, and share the joy of living one's dream.

My stage performance, afore mentioned, made me feel wonderful. I am high as a kite. It wasn't in a large or famous place. No press or celebrities or even monetary compensation. But I am so fulfilled, happy, soaring, accomplished. It is this positive result that makes me, and probably you and our friend Amelia, continue to follow our path. We want to continue enjoying, developing and soaring to new heights of accomplishments in the loving of that which is inborn in our soul and must be followed, resulting in explosive joy.

Author seeing if "I measure up to Amelia." Dress designed by Amelia, which is now displayed at her family home in Atchison, Kansas.

Author with Amelia's brand name luggage. Notice Amelia's birth home painted on the lamp.

Dear Reader . . .

Here are some suggestive thoughts to ponder and write in journaling this fun chapter.

How does fashion, fun and personal appearance weigh in on your job?

Do you find it unimportant, frivolous or troublesome?
Or do you enjoy it?

How do you apply creativity to your life to make home, job, hobbies, work best for you?

FLYING SUIT: LOOKING THE PART

Written December 2011

When beginning her flying lessons, Amelia took a leather jacket, rolled it around in dirt and oil to look worn like the other grease monkeys and fliers. She wore horse riding pants, or jodhpurs. These may have been a natural for her, since Amelia was an excellent horsewoman.

I was reading Giacinta Bradley Koontz' book, *Pioneer Mechanics in Aviation*, and saw a photo of a man dressed for flying. The suit was identical to Amelia's first suit!

Some early female fliers designed clothing based on the female couture styles of their day, or should we say the underwear of the day, as the look of bloomers were used as pants in place of the skirt. This was a very creative styling, sort of a culotte which has a cloth skirt-like panel in front of the pant-legs.

Early flier Harriet Quimby wore a purple satin bloomer style flight suit, looking glamorous and stylish on April 16, 1912, as she flew across the English Channel and other exploits.

Harriet Quimby (1875–1912). August 1, 1911, she became the first licensed female aviator in the United States.

In the 1920s and 30s women were fighting for equality and the right to vote. Wearing the same clothes as their male counterparts may have been a natural step or major statement as cutting one's hair.

Jodhpurs in their original shape. This is why I love investigating history. Jodhpurs are what early aviators wore, as did Amelia! Modern stretch fabrics eliminated the need for the hip wings.

Amelia Earhart seen here wearing jodhpurs.

Originally designed for horseback riding, jodhpurs were ideal for aviators.

CHAPTER THREE
FRIENDS AND FAMILY

FRIENDSHIPS

Written March 6, 2012 11:39 am

Photos: Bronze statue of Amelia Earhart "Forest of Friendship" Atchison, Kansas.

I'm all happy. I just talked with a friend, had a laugh or two, shared interesting news. Commonality, similar energy, interests and lifestyle bond one with lifelong friends.

Did Amelia have such female friendships?

Amelia had close male friends, such as Gene Vidal. Were those relationships sexual? There is no definitive evidence.

Amelia did have female friends. Were those relationships sexual? Again, there is no conclusive evidence to point in that direction.

Her cousin, Nancy Morse, said Amelia "was a loner . . . She had seen so much change in her childhood – she'd lived in many different places, she'd gone to many different schools" due to her father's job as a lawyer for the railroads. She attended 16 different schools.[1]

In her writings, Earhart does mention some ladies as friends. There was Louise Thaden, who married and gave up flying, much to Amelia's chagrin. Amelia believed that a woman should have the freedom to pursue her dreams. "If you are the first woman to fuel an urge in that direction, fuel it and act it. It may turn out to be fun and to me fun is the indispensable part of work."[2] A statement for which she was criticized in the press . . . the "fun" part, go figure.

Most of Amelia's friends were fliers and competitors. I have heard that best friends are often people one admires – and with whom one is competitive.

Photo : Friends L to R : Rhonda Towne, Author Roberta Bassin, Giacinta Bradley Koontz (Aviation Historian) taken at Amelia Earhart Festival, Atchison, Kansas

Dear Reader . . .

Are your friends people you admire, and yet do you find yourself somewhat competitive?

Do you think that is a good thing? Share your thoughts.

AMELIA AND HER MOM

Written March 21, 2011

My Mother died August 24, 2009 at age ninety-six and a half. When it is your own loved one, no life is ever long enough.

My mother died in a nursing home, a place she lived in for three and a half years because I was fearful that she wouldn't have been safe or well taken care of enough in her own home with only a live-in caretaker and myself visiting as often as possible. I feared that due to dementia, she would have screamed so loudly that the neighbors, one in particular, would have reported or called the cops, and she would have been placed into something called "lockdown."

Or, as the caretaker feared, she could possibly be reported mistakenly for abusing my mother when screams were heard coming from the little pink and white house.

I was advised by the social worker that the best option was a skilled nursing facility where there would be more pairs of eyes watching, more activity and less chance of abuse.

I was an only child. Amelia Earhart was not. The mother-daughter relationship, particularly for an only child of a single parent, is especially unique. One becomes more of a friend. There is a strange equality, tremendous attention, over protection (at least I felt that way). Being an only child, for me, was sometimes like living in a bubble.

Ironically, I kept my mother in a bubble, also. I was so worried she wouldn't be cared for properly, safely, that I put her in what I saw as an ultra protective environment with tons of staff. She could not be relaxed and happy as she would have been in her own home, except in the garden that she sat in for hours outside on the patio of her room.

A trusted friend said that if I took mother out of the nursing home, I might not be able to get her back in. Moreover, that any caretaker I hired might leave, perhaps without notice and that I would be running to her home to care for her, which I did anyway. You know what? Continuing to do for mother in her own home would have been like always. Maybe if I had not made the decision to put her into the nursing home, I would not feel the lingering guilt that I do feel to this day. Taking care of Mom was my job, which I was used to doing. It was a difficult adjustment for me, worse for her, not to run to her home to check up on her, have tea, talk, clean, cook, take her for an outing.

There was no good way with no good answer. I did what I thought was best at the time. Dealing with a similar situation presents a dilemma for each person.

Amelia's mother, Amy Earhart and Amelia Mary Earhart.

Author's mother, Sally Kaufman and Author, Roberta Bassin.

TAKING CARE OF FAMILY

Written August 25 (year undated)

We, Amelia and I, both have a strong sense of family, a dedication to family and friends.

Amelia was an avid writer, sending many letters to her mother:

> August 12, 1928
> "Sent package to P (Pidge aka Muriel). Hope she can use things. If you know something she wants get it for her and I'll pay. Also you. My treat, at last."[3]

I find this letter so telling. This was soon after her sudden rise in notoriety and income since becoming the first female to cross the Atlantic by air.

It just reminded me of when I got my first major film role. I smile as I remember how good it felt to be able to treat my mother and Aunt Lil to a Las Vegas Holiday, including a dinner show to see one of their favorite performers, Englebert Humperdinck. Wow, so long ago! Thank you again Amelia, for reminding me.

Another example of Amelia's generosity, dated August 28, 1928:

> Please throw away rags and get things you need on my account. I'll instruct them. I can do it now and the pleasure is mine.
> Yr. doter
> A[4]

(Interestingly, noted here, before the advent of "texting and emailing," our Amelia, many times in her casual personal notes, abbreviated words as you see changing "your daughter" to "yr. doter." I think this was not only for economy but also attributable to her playful nature, which gets overshadowed by her fame, her shyness and her ultimate unfortunate demise.)

I so enjoy her letters since they are a true look into her mindset. I almost feel a little guilty, as these were intended for the sender and receivers' eyes only. Amelia was very careful about what she let the public know and see regarding her private life. Sadly, a huge repository of her personal correspondence and artifacts, including poems she wrote from her school days, was lost in a fire at the Putnam home in Rye, New York, in November 1934.

FINANCES

Written (year undated)

Even as a young girl at The Ogontz School for Young Ladies, Amelia was frugal, making a little go a long way as when she bought a pair of used shoes.

October 1916 from a letter to her mother while attending school in Philadelphia:

> I hate to spend money for things I never will need nor want. I bought a pair of Leonora's black high-heeled slippers. They fit me and I needed some and she didn't like them so I bot them for five dollars.
> > Lots of Love,
> > Mill[5]

Amelia was critical of her family members who did not manage money well. Amelia's concern for her family's finances is demonstrated in another letter written in the fall of 1931:

> Dear Mother,
> I do not mean to be harsh, but I know the family failing about money. It is true that I have a home and food but what I send yu is what I myself earn and it does not come from GP.
> > Yr. Doter
> > A[6]

In this realm, our families and experiences differ. I admired my mother and aunt for managing finances so well, having little and making it go a long way. I learned from them. To this day I marvel at how well they did without ever making me feel I had to go without. In fact, I always seemed to appreciate everything they did for me, giving me dance and violin lessons, an art easel and paints . . . nurturing any talent they saw I was interested in exploring. With any monetary gifts given to me, my mother would say, "We'll put this in the bank for when you go to UCLA." There was no question that I was going to university. Of course, UCLA is my alma mater, and I owe it all to my mother's attitude that a college education was simply a "matter of fact."

Nevertheless, Amelia's financial outlook may help make others aware of their own history and dealings with monetary issues.

Dear Reader . . .

Take a moment and jot down your thoughts about finances.

How does your family's financial history affect your current money management style? Interesting, isn't it?

AMELIA'S CONCERN FOR HER MOTHER'S HEALTH

Written September 26, 2013

Amelia's letter to her mother, dated approximately July 1935:

> What do you mean your throat? What sense is there in
> neglecting health? You know I want you to be treated whenever
> necessary. See a doctor and write me. You may be a menace to
> the children besides yourself. I never heard of such stuff!!!!!!!
> X?X---[7]

I so relate to Amelia's frustration as the child becomes the parent.
I remember feeling this way when my mother didn't want to go to the
doctor, take her pills, or do her exercises.

It has been four and a half years (at the time of this entry) since my
mother left this world. I am older, maybe wiser or just guilt-ridden or
romanticizing the past, but my new outlook is that I should have not
been so insistent. I should have allowed my parent to do or not do what
she wanted.

At ninety-four or ninety-five, with some dementia, when I would try
to get my mother to do her physical therapy, she would say, "I'm old,"
with a tone meaning leave me alone, there is no reason to do them. And
you know that can be a reason, even a viable excuse in itself.

It is true that I constantly blame myself for Mother's not having lived a
few more days or longer, even in a deteriorating condition. As I write
this, I know she would not have lived as long as she did had I not taken
many steps and interceded on many occasions to get her to the doctor
for certain medical tests. For instance, one of the tests that she said she
would not submit to, discovered she had a blood problem. Maybe she
just wanted me to push her to show my concern. Nevertheless, I did
what I thought was best with the best of intentions to keep her well, if
not happy.

I did, like Amelia, try to keep my mother happy, by buying her gifts and visiting her all the time. Now I realize I did what I thought was needed, not what she wanted. She wanted me just to sit and talk with her in her home, not to be cleaning house, which I now see that I often did out of nervousness.

Not until she was in the nursing facility, where I couldn't do anything else but sit and talk to her, did I go from obligation to loving her.

She always questioned my love for her.

Two days before she died, on a beautiful summer spring-like day, sitting on the large patio in the shade of a large full green cypress bush outside her skilled nursing room, she said in a pleasant, contented voice, "This is nice."

I smiled, I felt relaxed, content, and connected seated angular beside her. Leaning slightly toward her, I said, "I love you."

She replied, "I know."

I asked, "Should I have done everything to keep you going?"

Her response, "Yes."

I guess somehow we both knew it was over.

I'm so glad she acknowledged that. Her mind was alert on that visit. One could always tell when things were right and when they weren't. But on this afternoon all was okay.

Why I can't let go of all my guilt, I don't know. I remember when on one visit to the facility, I told her "I worry about you all the time."

Her reply, "Why?"
She would not have wanted me to be sad or guilt-ridden but rather to enjoy each day.

For herself, she wanted to live as long as possible.

I tell myself, "I did my best." We all do. I did my best at the time, with the situation, given my own personality, her personality, information, lack of information. The list is endless. The answer to the question "What is best for my loved one?" is non answerable . . . a conundrum.

Dear Reader . . .

What is your conundrum, my dear reader?

Please share your thoughts and experiences.

We all need to be supportive of one another. I hope in opening my heart to you, you can open your heart to Amelia and Me.

ARGUMENTS

Family
Written July 20, 2013

Did Amelia have arguments with her family members as all other families do? You bet. Letters show that indeed she did. "Discussions" as I call them. My son calls the same discussions arguments. For example, Amelia, being protective, was not going to let her mother be used by her sister Muriel to care for her children, in addition to caring for her sister's house. Amelia laid down the law.

Letter dated June 8, 1933
Rye, NY

> Dear Mother,
>   I wired you from Cleveland where I had flown in a test hop. I did not want you to arrange to go to some Maine dump that none of us knew anything about when there are so many places that are available and better situated.
>   In the first place you are not to have both children. If you have David part of the time I cannot object but two is out of the question and I will not permit under any circumstances. You are not the kind of woman who has no other interest but brats and I do not see the necessity of your being a drudge and nurse maid . . . [8]

Another letter not only demonstrates typical family strife, but also Amelia's vulnerable side.

November 4, 1932
New York

> Dear Mother,
>   I just returned from Chicago and points west where I have had one of the first of my lectures. Everything went well. I flew and trained when necessary and did not attempt to go so far by car.

I shall be here ten days and then start out in New England. GP is going with me to the most northern points as I do not like the territory very well as you know and need moral support.

I don't know what to say about you accompanying. I thought from one crack you made that you didn't really care to go. You said maybe it was just as well that you didn't go so there could be no chance of your disgracing me or words to that effect. However, there may be ways yet if you want to for a few days, and I try to work something out.[9]

COMPETITION FOR MY LOYALTY

Written July 14, 2013

Who was competing for my love, my loyalty? Were they competing, my mother and aunt?

Since I was a child, was I manipulated without knowing it?
Now as an older adult, I am still experiencing guilt about disrespecting my mother's memory by possibly making my Aunt Lill's memorial plaque larger than Mother's.

Originally I didn't set out with any thought in mind other than to add a more complete description of the specialness of my auntie. Cousin Helen had said Lill was "good natured and full of fun." From that time on I wanted to add that statement to her memorial plaque. On Lill's birthday, I finally felt moved to do so and wrote a new memorial. But I felt motivated to add even more. I wanted to add that Lill was more than just my aunt, recognizing that, as she herself said, "I was a mother too." Sadly her infant son had died, which made her no less a mother. So I added exactly that, "Young wife and mother too."

Then I thought about how generous she was monetarily and felt this should be added along with "good natured and full of fun."
Finally, I signed it with "Love you."

I didn't realize at the time; actually I didn't realize until a few days ago, that this plaque may be larger than the one for my mother. My dilemma then became: what should I do? Is it important to make the plaques exactly the same size? I've worked my whole life not to hurt my mother because she feared, "You love your aunt more than me." Now I had innocently made a plaque, which I had not yet approved, that for all eternity could be interpreted as just what I worked so hard to avoid.

But as I write this I realize that it isn't so. This is just a plaque about my aunt and the best of her. Whether she as a human being did things to make me love her, perhaps because she was competitive with my mom,

I do not know, but in the end, I know they both vied for my affection and love because they both loved me so much. Just good, good people, flawed as we all are, but really the best.

Mother didn't know how to show or to gain love, so she did it backwards, saying "You won't take care of me the way you take care of your aunt," instead of just asking me or knowing that I would.

What to do, what to do about the plaque?

A final note: today, June 16, 2014, one year later, the plaque is up. I visited and it made me happy. No guilt. I have no regrets about this. I looked up at it. I could see it from a distance. It was the right decision.

Thank you dear readers for allowing me to share with you.

Dear Reader . . .

Did Amelia have conflicts like this?

Was there competition between her and her sister for their parents' and grandparents' love and visa versa?

What about your own childhood?

Does this resonate with you, and how?

PROTECTION OF FAMILY, MARRIAGE

A Comparison of this author and our Amelia and maybe you too.
Written August 5, 2013

I protected her, my Mom.
Amelia took care of her Mom too.

I was an only child.
Amelia was a first born.
The same thing (or so psychologists purport)
You feel responsible for the family.
I took care of my aunt too out of love.

Amelia took care of her mother, Amy. Was it out of love or
responsibility or obligation? I took care of my mother until I didn't feel I
could safely have her in her own home. Amelia was building a house in
Toluca Lake with separate quarters for her mother.

When she was at home, I felt I took care of my mother Sally, out of
obligation. When she was in the skilled nursing facility, and my hands-
on duties were fewer, I then learned, oddly, to feel love for her. Like me,
Amelia always felt responsible for her immediate family.

Amelia came from a divorced family with a problematic father.
Educated to be a lawyer, Edwin Earhart was an alcoholic. He
disappointed her many times, but he was there trying to make a living.
Her parents divorced when Amelia was an adult.

Me, I came from a divorced – or as they used to call it – "broken home."
My father left the day I was born, which sounds horrible. But now I
consider the circumstances. He was educated to be a chemist. He had
problems having been severely shell shocked in World War II. He
disappointed my mother and me. She worked at making sure I knew I
had a father by having me write letters to him to which he responded.
She never spoke angrily about him. I always admired how she handled
the situation telling me many good events in their life together.

I met him once when I was five. I remember it so clearly. We walked up a cement walkway with a nicely manicured front lawn. The house was two story, painted white, with some light colored trim, a classic home of maybe the 1920s. However, his apartment was unlike any way of living I had ever seen. My mother and aunt had managed to buy a lovely home, new furniture, in an up and coming California neighborhood.

This one room apartment seemed strange, foreign. I had never seen someone living in such surroundings – with a standing metal closet. It just didn't seem like a pleasant way to reside. It defined his lifestyle to me: lonely, removed, unadorned, empty, lacking warmth.

His appearance was slim, with loose fitting clothes of the times, not old, nor new, just 40s style. This was 1953, I was five. That is how I remember it.

But unlike Amelia's father, when I was twelve, my father filed for custody. He did not consider what was best for me. That I was with a stable, loving, care-giving family of my mother and aunt.

My disappointment erupted. My mother welcomed him into our home. I even had them dance a waltz, wanting, hoping to form a traditional family again. I invited him to my sixth grade graduation. We went shopping for shoes, which he bought me saying, "I didn't know women's shoes cost so much." Then out of the blue, he filed for full custody. The tide had turned. I saw him not as a possibility of a loving father, but only as a biological father. I no longer wanted this person as a part of our lives. It is a sad commentary resulting from his own actions.

He would stare at me. This stayed with me for years. He would walk in front of our home calling my name. My mother would have me safely spend weekends at my Uncle Joey's with my cousins. Finally, a restraining order was issued.

Amelia and I both came from divorced families which influenced our outlook at marriage.

Amelia's "reluctance to marry GP" or anyone was, as she said, due to "My parents' unhappy marriage and my need for freedom (which) set little trust in this institution (marriage)."[10]

Unlike Amelia, I did not witness a bad marriage growing up, but I did see how unhappy both Mother and Auntie were, not to have a marriage; even though my mother would sometimes say, "it's better to be alone than be with the wrong person." Amelia would probably agree, "Being alone is scary, but not as scary as feeling alone in a relationship."

Thus my mother wanted me to marry young, not to risk losing the right person.

I was determined to work at making a good marriage and setting a good example for my children of a stable traditional household.

In the end, both Amelia and I took on the responsibility, care, obligation and attachment to our families along with forming strong marital unions.

Dear Reader . . .

YOUR THOUGHTS: Friends, Family, Marriage . . .

How do you relate or respond to Amelia's care ethic, her outlook on marriage, women's need for freedom and financial dealings?

Are there similarities of your outlook?

How do you differ?

Enjoy sharing and just jotting down your ideas.

Chapter Four

Weak Constitution, Strong Determination

WHEN ALL IS GOING GREAT . . . OOPS

Written March 2, 2012

"When all is going very well indeed, it's time to anticipate trouble, and conversely, when all seems sour beyond words, a break lurks just around the corner,"[1] was the quote of Amelia's that immediately came to mind after I had my car accident.

> We had planned on a dawn start from Honolulu on our round-the-world flight. So easily was the airplane going down the concrete runway, I thought the takeoff was actually over. Ten seconds later, the airplane lay helpless on the runway, a broken bird with battered wings. I don't know what happened.[2]

I had a fender bender accident yesterday, March 1, 2012 on Malibu Canyon Road. The day before, I thought to myself, ". . . so nice, my car looks great, not like that bent up license plate on another car I saw." I was feeling physically better than I had in a long time – "menopausal zest" the gals at one of my best friend's birthday party, which I had been attending that day, called it.

Then on the way home, feeling tired, on a slow moving wait at the stop light, lost in thought and glancing to look at my purse and water bottle, I was taken aback by a sudden light jolt.

Realizing I had hit the pickup truck in front of me, I saw him pull over, I did the same. He had no damage that I saw. I turned to look at my car and much to my surprise, "Oh my gosh," the bumper had lifted off and was separated from the car, with a piece hanging off. Much to my chagrin, there was my license plate looking just like that horrible one that had so appalled me earlier. Hmmmm. Never be critical. Right.

On her first round-the-world flight attempt, Amelia's quotation regarding her own accident taking off from Honolulu, the Electra swerving and damaging the plane, came to mind.

Amelia said, "I don't know what happened." I said, "How did I do that?" I really didn't know, and I'm still not really sure how that accident happened.

In defense of Amelia, I now can see how one doesn't always know exactly "what happened and how." Also, Amelia was visibly shaken – and rightly so. I was surprised to find that even I, with this minor accident, was a little disoriented, fumbling for the information to give to the other driver, tripping over a small mound of dirt as I walked to my car door. I even forgot to write down the other person's license number as we used our cell phone cameras to get all the information in this new age of technology . . . sigh.

WEAK CONSTITUTION BUT
GOING FORWARD

Written September 4, 2011 7:28 a.m.

I feel tired, my back is tired, I'm a little hungry and sleepy, and it is only 8:30 in the morning!

Imagine Amelia flying and feeling this way – only worse.

A woman with a weak constitution but a strong determination – that best describes Amelia Earhart.

> "To want in one's head to do a thing, for it's own sake: to enjoy doing it: to concentrate all of one's energies upon it, that is not only the surest guarantee of it's success; it is also being true to oneself," Amelia had stated.[3]

This philosophy kept her going as violent storms beat the paint off her Lockheed Electra flying over Karachi and India, and I am sure on the last leg of her round-the-world flight. "Push through, we're always pushing through," wrote Amelia.[4]

Husband George and friend Gene Vidal implored Amelia to abort the flight at Lae, New Guinea, concerned that her navigator Fred Noonan was drinking. According to Gene Vidal's son, Gore, Amelia said, "Oh I think it will be alright."[5] She chose to continue the flight – to unresolved and disastrous results.

I see myself. I relate to this strongly. My aunt called me "the forcer." Remembering a decision which continues to haunt me. I insisted on taking my mother out. Mom said, "maybe we shouldn't go." I said, "no no, let's go." And like Amelia, to disastrous results. We had a car accident. My mother, age ninety three and four months, broke both her legs, resulting in undue pain, suffering, and ultimately forcing her to live her remaining three years in a skilled nursing facility, a guilt I carry to this day.

Like Amelia, I cared for my family, and like Amelia, with strong insistence, caring sometimes too much. Taking control and being on top of every decision regarding my Mother's health, perhaps taking charge too much. The burden, the blessing, the drive to get it right, do it right, make it work, do it all, sometimes backfires in our face.

How does this happen, one asks? Because, 99% of the time, that take-charge, passionate, go-for-it attitude provides positive results. With the same vigor and determination, I got myself to my dance class when I realized I was running late having been absorbed in writing this entry. A little comedic relief.

DID AMELIA EVER HAVE HEADACHES?

Written July 28, 2013

I have a headache this morning. Probably from the stress of a little tiff with my son last night, or maybe just because I waited too long to eat breakfast (which I often do). I had gone on the computer, followed by exercising and finally eating after getting up at 5:54 a.m. It is now 8:45 a.m. I just finished my good-girl healthy oatmeal with brown sugar and fresh blueberries, hot tea and eight naughty little soda crackers (unsalted duly noted.)

Amelia often missed meals when she was about to fly, as before her solo Atlantic flight, "No time for luncheon" when GP called to inform her of "perfect flying weather."

> As fast as I dared, traffic cops being what they are, I drove the 25 miles home to Rye. Five minutes was enough to pick up a few things and a lingering few more to drink in the beauty of the Dogwood Tree beneath our bedroom window. Those sweet blooms wished me a fond farewell. That is a memory I shall never forget. As for the difficulty of long flights, if one is in good condition, one needs little food and little sleep. On my solo Atlantic flight, I took no change of clothes and sipped one can of tomato (pronounced short 'a' British style) juice during the fifteen-hour flight.[6]

Does that answer the question?

Of course Amelia had a queasy stomach, and there were plenty of fumes, rocky ups and downs and just plain inactivity on long flights in 1932. So eating really doesn't appear to be very appetizing during flights.

But looking at her, she is always very lean. She did eat a "whole chicken" after a long flight. I don't get the impression that eating was a major source of pleasure or indulgence. It was just what was necessary.

Oops, did I get sidetracked? I meant to be answering the question: did Amelia get headaches, not did she eat.

Definitely! Amelia suffered from chronic sinus infections, which probably meant she got headaches. She was operated on for this condition at Cedars Sinai hospital a number of times, getting her sinuses drained. This did not stop her from following her passion of flying. She persevered.

INDECISION

Written August 29, 2013

I am trying to decide if I should go with a new manager. I lie awake in bed weighing the pros and cons, thinking, thinking, and thinking. Even after a decision is made, I probably will question it. That's me.

But as my career coach, Dallas Travers says, over thinking or "trying to achieve perfection is just a form of procrastination," which I do not see in Amelia's personality, but I do see in mine.

Would some over thinking have saved her from her fatal flight? Or do we still make the same decisions whether we over-think or not? "Obviously I faced the possibility of not returning when first I considered going. Once faced and settled there really wasn't any good reason to refer to it," Amelia so frankly stated.[7]

In Amelia's case, I think GP and Amelia knew all the facts. Whether they chose "to ignore some basic facts," as Brad Washburn, interviewed to be her navigator, said, will always be up for debate. Did they risk too much in their quest to complete their scheduled July 4th arrival date, and round-the-world flight book launch, for the Christmas sales? We will never know.

But we have to agree, Amelia made strong decisions, and followed through without second guessing herself, never regretful or looking back. A lesson many of us need to implement.

On the other hand, one might also be reminded to discern when to stick to our guns and when to let "discretion" be "the better part of valor."

Thus, there is much to mull over.

Dear Reader . . .

Are there decisions you are having trouble making?

Writing them out may help.

Have you ever made a decision that you later regretted, seeing in hindsight that all the signs were there and that you should NOT have followed through?

What do you do with your feelings about such decisions?

PHYSICAL PROBLEMS DIDN'T STAND IN HER WAY

Written June 1, 2013

Sinus, backache, stomach problems, Amelia Earhart had them all. I am reminded this morning as I awoke experiencing the trio, but physical discomfort didn't stop her from making the improbable, uncomfortable, impractical, illogical choice of being a long distance "stunt " aviator. The thrill, the joy, the interest had to be fueled with the dream of flying high in the sky.

Amelia's poem entitled "Courage" exemplifies her philosophy:

COURAGE

> Courage is the price that life exacts for granting peace.
> The soul that knows it not knows no release from little things.
> Knows not the livid loneliness of fear nor mountain heights
> Where bitter joy can hear the sound of wings.
>
> How can life grant us boon of living?
> Compensate for dull gray ugliness and pregnant hate?
> Unless we dare the soul's dominion?
>
> Each time we make a choice,
> We pay with courage,
> to behold resistless day and count it fair.[8]

Amelia, especially in this poem, gives me the encouragement to do what I want but find difficult, fearful and uncomfortable. I am reminded not to let these inhibitions stop me. It frees me to experience all that is interesting, enriching and gloriously wonderful, whether as simple as flying (I'm a white knuckle flier . . . surprise!) to see my little grandson, or performing before thousands of people.

It is the joy of the ride. As in acting, when the character takes me on a ride and I know I have "nailed it," so Amelia loved being up in the clouds: "For me flying was a sport not a circus . . . I appeared in public only on special occasions . . . alone to be enjoyed," a personal enjoyment.[9]

Today, March 12, 2014, as I happen to read this entry, I am dealing with this exact dilemma. Once again, Amelia's words are helping me push forward to pursue my dreams. In this case, to write my *Amelia Earhart Self Help Book* which is, ironically, helping me and I hope it is of help to you, my readers, as well.

Dear Reader . . .

Write down your goals, big or small, for today or the future.

Jot down what may be in your way either physically and/or emotionally.

Take a moment to think of Amelia's determination and courage and the exhilaration you feel with just doing anything towards reaching your goal.

I know you will feel better, as I do, having taken another step forward. I feel the smile.

CHAPTER FIVE

THE RELATIONSHIP

George Palmer Putnam & Amelia Earhart

WEDDING ANNIVERSARY

Anniversary
Written August 27, 2011

Today is my anniversary of forty-four years (at the time this was written; now it's 52 and better than ever in all realms . . . ha ha). I had a storybook wedding; well, it was *my* storybook wedding.

Just the opposite of Amelia's wedding. It was held at George's mother's home in Noank, Connecticut. "After the wedding, I wired my sister Muriel, over the broomstick with GP. Break the news gently to Mother."[1] Thus apparently, no guests, not even Amelia's mother and sister.

Amelia wore a brown dress, as seen here in her wedding portrait, took no honeymoon, and went right back to work the next day.

Did George love Amelia or was it just a partnership for profit?

Originally the young woman was a skeptical bride. Amelia married in 1931 "Doubtful of my own ability to cope with matrimony. My parents' unhappy marriage and my need for freedom set doubt in this institution." On the morning of her wedding, February 7, 1931, she handed George a letter:[2]

```
                                        Noank
                                        Connecticut


                    The Square House
                    Church Street



Dear GPP

              There are some things which should be writ before
we are married -- things we have talked over before -- most of
them.

              You must know again my reluctance to marry, my
feeling that I shatter thereby chances in work which means most
to me.  I feel the move just now as foolish as anything I
could do.  I know there may be compensations but have no heart
to look ahead.

              On our  life together I want you to understand I
shall not hold you to any midaevil code of faithfulness to me
nor shall I conider myself bound to you similarly.  If we can
be honest I think the difficulties which arise may best be avoided
should you or I become interested deeply (or in passing) in anyone
else.

              Please let us not interfere with the others' work or
play, nor let the world see our private joys or disagreements.
In this connection I may have to keep some place where I can go to
be myself, now and then, for I cannot guarantee to endure at all
times the confinement of even an attractive cage.

              I must exact a cruel promise and that is you will let
me go in a year if we find no happiness together.

              I will try to do my best in every way and give you that
part  of me you know and seem to want.

                                        A.E.
```

It was 1931, Amelia was thirty-three years old, had never planned to marry and thought it "foolish as anything I could do."

The following letter from George Palmer Putnam to Amelia dated 1937
(Purdue Archives):

"I want peace – and you. I'm never really content anymore when
I'm away from you . . . please love me a lot."

Another letter dated March 27, 1937 (Purdue Archives) to a woman
named Helen after crash in Honolulu on Amelia's first attempt to
circumnavigate the globe, George writes:

"As for me, I've urged her to do just what she wants to. I'd like
it if she quit. But she won't. So my job is clear – to help her all I
can."

AMELIA'S MARRIAGE BEGINS

Written (undated)

In February, as she began married life, she wrote her mother:

N.Y. Feb. 22, 1931

I am much happier than I expected I could ever be in that
state. I believe the whole thing was for the best. Of course I go
on in the same way as before as far as business is concerned. I
haven't changed at all and will only be busier I suppose . . .

I want you to come over as soon as you wish and the
apartment [at 42W. 58th St]. I have two canaries and you know
I've wanted one for ever so long. You can stay here at the hotel
in another room. If the cousins want to come they can be here
too . . .

I sent Muriel the $2500 promised. I hope it will mean a lot to
her, moving into a decent house. I can't see Medford anywhere,
however, with Albert's biz in Cambridge, etc. When are you
going there, do you know? I am asking Pidge down here, maybe
we could have a blowout together before she becomes tied down
– or is it obvious too late for her?

Write your plans.

Yr. doter,

A[3]

Amy was not happy about her daughter's marriage to a divorced man ten years her senior with two children, and not the most likable of people, or so it was rumored. It took Amy six months to finally visit the married couple.

Marriage was not in Amelia's original plans, having refused George many times. Even telling the press ". . . no marriage plans," but secretly she had decided to accept.

I, on the other hand, married just after I turned nineteen years old, had a formal religious ceremony with friends and family, and, as described by a young cousin, "a huge gown with a long train." I just loved it. Bridesmaids in turquoise and all the trimmings, and my mother was, as someone suggested, "getting married again."

Amelia had been married for seven years at the time of her disappearance, but there were rumblings of dissatisfaction in year six. Possibly the grind of staying in the limelight didn't help.

However, they were both very driven people and forged an amazing team. As Putnam's granddaughter, Sally Chapman, said, "But in fact, she (Amelia) knew what she wanted and knew this man could get the job done."[4]

MALE ATTRACTION

Written Sept 12, 2011 6:38 p.m.

"I met the cutest boy," I said, to my mom and aunt upon having just met my future husband. I was jumping up-and-down and side-to-side, to my mother and aunt sitting on the couch. What were they thinking? Me home from a holiday social and all bubbly about some boy I'd just met. And he was just a boy. He was only nineteen and I was seventeen and a half (halves are still important at that age).

Amelia may not have been jumping up-and-down or bouncing side-to-side when she met George Palmer Putnam, but she was aware of some attraction to this high powered publisher, as apparently were other women, his having married four times. Ironically, Amelia related, GP "looked at me as if I were a sack of potatoes upon our first meeting."[5]

A very rare interview with Amelia a few years after their initial meeting tells the story. (p.153 "Sound of Wings," possibly from periodical *The Illustrated Love Magazine*, January 1932.)

> I had no special feelings about Mr. Putnam at first. I was too absorbed in the prospects of the trip and of my being the one to make it . . . of course after I had talked to him for very long I was conscious of the brilliant mind and keen insight of the man . . .

Upon staying at George's home at Rye, New York, Amelia wrote her book, "*20 Hrs. 40 Min.: Our Flight in the Friendship.*"

> Mr. Putnam and I found that we had many things in common; I was interested in aviation, so was he. We both loved the outdoors, books and sports. And so we lunched together, and dined together, took long horseback rides together. Usually we were surrounded by many people, both he and I had many friends and were invited to the same parties. We came to depend on each other, yet it was only friendship between us, or so – at least – I thought at first. At least I didn't admit even to myself that I was in love . . . but at last the time came, I don't quite

know when it happened, when I could deceive myself no longer. I couldn't continue telling myself that what I felt for GP was only friendship. I knew I had found the one person who could put up with me.

Amelia and I came from families where our parents' marriages did not work out, ending in divorce. Similarly, this affected our view of marriage, but in very different ways.

In my case, I vowed and told my then prom and grad night date (now husband), "We must always talk about everything (which of course has never materialized due to the typical nature of his male brain) and that the word *divorce* was to never be mentioned." The latter dictum being based on the idea that once the word is out there, the floodgates have been opened, and the possibility is a possibility. I was determined to make my marriage work. Marriage does take work, mutual respect and commitment on the part of both partners.

August 27th 1967, at the ripe old age of two months into nineteen years of age, I Roberta Ellen Kaufman took Ned Franklin Bassin, age twenty-one, both still students at University of California at Los Angeles, to be wedded husband and wife. We said our "I do's" in a princess-for-a-day dream-like religious ceremony before family and friends.

Amelia took the opposite approach. She avoided marriage for a long time, finally accepting GP's last proposal and exchanging vows in the simplest of no-frills ceremonies.

From the *New York Times* Dated February 7, 1931:

Got License on Nov. 8

Mrs. Putnam Sr. said today that the engagement dated back about three months, and that it was not until last night that she was informed that they were to be married today.

"They telephoned me from New York and told me they would be married here today," she said. "Then they motored out last night and made arrangements with Judge Anderson, a friend of the family."

"There was no fuss, no religious ceremony, no demonstration," said Mrs. Putnam, pointing out that the house contained no flowers, and that no one in the neighborhood had been informed. Brown shoes and stockings and a close-fitting brown hat were worn by Miss Earhart in addition to her brown traveling suit. Brown, it seems, is her favorite color. Mrs. Putnam Sr. wore a gray Canton crepe housedress, and Mr. Putnam and the other men wore business attire.

Different points of view, different philosophies in dealing with dysfunctional family backgrounds, but in both cases, happy partnerships resulted.

OUR MATES

Written September 28, 2013

Were we just lucky or wise? Did we both lay out a plan, a check list?

All of Amelia's letters, notes, and references point to her adverse feelings and total lack of necessity for a committed relationship.

In her youth, her beau and trusted friend was Sam Chapman. In 1928, he was entrusted with the secret of Amelia's upcoming flight as a passenger across the Atlantic. Upon takeoff, as Amelia instructed, Sam was to inform her mother Amy of her daughter's flight. However, the press broke it to her mother Amy before Sam could notify her.[6]

Chapman wanted a traditional marriage, but that wasn't Amelia's point of view. "I don't want to tell Sam what he should do," said Amelia regarding Sam's job, to her sister Muriel. "He ought to know what makes him happiest, and then do it, no matter what other people say. I know what I want to do and I expect to do it, married or single!" Eventually, the six-year engagement was called off.[7]

I don't think marriage was in her plans. She probably surprised herself by later agreeing to marry George Palmer Putnam.

From the photos, film footage and letters it appears very strongly that Amelia was attracted to George physically and mentally. They had the same interests, goals, and adventuresome spirit. He had been an explorer in the Arctic and a sheriff in the still undeveloped Oregon territory. He was the best publicist in the business and would make her the most famous woman of the twentieth century, earning an unheard of income for speaking tours.

"I went from earning just enough to pay for my lessons (flying) to accumulating fifty-thousand dollars from various avenues of employment. This involved twenty-seven lectures a month, eight articles a year for *Cosmopolitan*, and promotions," Amelia said, as a result of being the first female passenger to successfully cross the Atlantic.[8]

Amelia found some of this notoriety humorous: "Why one should be considered an expert in a totally foreign field because of their fame is beyond me."[9]

Ironically and sadly, this same drive for adventure, achievement and monetary accumulation, which seems to be a joint effort, as stated by GP's granddaughter Sally Cartwright, may have been the cause of the ill-fated "Last Flight."

The Putnam's long range goals, which overshadowed their decisions regarding the round-the world flight, is further exemplified in an account by Brad Washburn, who was being considered as the navigator. Brad recalled, "I pointed out to her and Putnam two problems. You've got to get a radio on Howland Island," making it a "cinch" to locate the tiny atoll. "But she didn't want to do it."

Washburn suggested strongly that Amelia carry low frequency radio equipment, enabling ships to locate her, which she refused to accept. Deferring to Putnam, Amelia asked, "What do you think?"[10]

June 12, 2001, in a newspaper interview, Washburn confided, "Well, I've never said this to anyone, but I may as well cough it up." GP said, at the time with regard to equipping the plane with a radio, "If you go to all that trouble the book [about the flight] will not be out for the Christmas sales."[11] Looks like the famous couple was of like minds.

I see I have veered off. Now how does my choice in mates relate to Amelia Earhart? I did have a checklist; I knew I wanted marriage, children, and a career in teaching and entertainment. Amelia and I definitely had different life plans in that regard. BUT, when we both were lucky enough to have these men come into our lives, we each recognized that these handsome, intelligent, like-minded, supportive individuals were right as team players and life partners.

Dear Reader . . .

Does Amelia and George's relationship make you think about your own?

Do you see any similarities?

Were they equal partners? Or did one dominate the other?

Do you choose relationships based on emotion, logic, or some combination?

Maybe you are involved in that dilemma as you read this chapter. I hope our journey sheds some helpful light.

Jot down a few thoughts.

Amelia and husband George
Palmer Putnam at the Hotel
Lotti, Paris France, 1932.

Author Roberta and
husband Ned Bassin
at Living Legends of
Aviation Gala – The
Beverly Hilton Hotel,
Beverly Hills, California

Dear Reader . . .

Can you think of relationships of which you didn't approve, but in the end, all seemed "for the best?"

How did you deal with this?

Share your thoughts.

WEDDING FRUSTRATIONS

Written July 26, 2013

This Saturday I'm attending my cousin's wedding. In fact, I am attending three weddings this summer. These are all relatively large costly affairs, requiring extensive planning and preparation. I enjoy these occasions but know they can be very stressful for the families prior to the event.

Amelia abhorred weddings. She went to her sister's reluctantly. Well, it may have been for different reasons, but I feel an overwhelming frustration that they cause schisms between the family hosting the wedding and those not invited who, I surmise, weren't important to the bride and groom in the first place. But it is the families of the partially invited, such as parents but not their adult children, a good friend instead of an uncle, that wreaks havoc with the relations.

Amelia disliked weddings, probably because of the formality, religiosity, and just the plain fuss of it all.

Letter Dated Feb. 13, 1933
Rye, NY

> Dear Mother,
> I am going to Chicago the end of this week for a wedding. I loathe the formal kind and have never attended any since Pidge got me inside a church for hers. (I don't mean only church weddings are awful, of course.)[12]

Well *I*, on the other hand, always loved weddings because of exactly that: the formality, religiosity and fuss. However, are all the hurt feelings, personal slights (most likely unintentional, just being practical as the betrothed see it) and lifelong dissension worth it?

As for the couple's view, they may have dreamt of a fabulous wedding, but to afford the wedding they want, they can only have a strict limit of guests, or even with unlimited funds, the venue of their dreams seats say four hundred people. Therefore, only four hundred of their dearest relatives and friends on both sides of the family can be invited, leaving everyone else seething with anger and swearing they will never invite the betrothed or their parents to anything again.

How does one reconcile this? My first inclination is simply not to mention the event to people who are not invited and hold my breath that they won't learn of the event, which of course they will. This may prompt one to call the host and ask them to make an exception for an extra guest, which they will most likely refuse to do.

A common reaction is to refuse to attend unless that special person is allowed to attend, which usually just leaves one out in the cold with the answer "So don't come," finding out you are not as valued as you thought.

Lastly, if two are invited, one of you can stay home, having the injured person go in their stead. Still not making for a pleasant situation.

There are many ways brides, grooms, families who are planning weddings approach such minefields. All of them, however, are pretty graceless and may result in fractured relationships.

Woe is me. There is no good solution other than after making sure no mistake has been made, just declining due to a "conflict" (pun intended) and sending a gift to show you want to continue the relationship on a positive note.

I don't like any of these options; I just want my uninvited to be invited. I can insist on including everyone by stomping my foot and whining about it or by taking it in my stride and accepting that weddings are difficult and there are always limits.

I know, let's celebrate, and have a block party inviting one and all!

Dear Reader . . .

What are your thoughts about how people decide whom to invite (and not invite) to their or their child's wedding?

Have you dealt with this social difficulty?

Any suggestions?

DID AMELIA AND GEORGE GET INTO RIDICULOUS LITTLE ARGUMENTS?

Written August 14, 2012?

Last night, well actually 2 a.m. after staying up to film our first at-home self-taped audition, we got into bed. Having an audition that morning at 11:30 a.m., and going to bed sooo late, I said laughingly, "Maybe we ought to set the alarm for 9:30 a.m., but I don't want it to wake you."

Ned, in a whiny upset voice, said, "Oh, do you want it set or not?"

"Well, I just don't want you to have to wake up early," I responded.

"Ro, don't keep going on about this," he said.

"I just don't understand you" I countered.

"That's right, keep it going," raising his voice a little. (Keep in mind that we are both lying flat on our backs in a king size bed countering each other at two in the morning.)

"I just want to be considerate, and you get angry! I don't understand you," I said in frustration.

He growled, whined something.

I said, "All right set the alarm."

He did. I turned away, thinking things over and very sad. I had just been thinking how great it was that we had worked together so well, almost in a professional manner, to have filmed this little audition, and now, to my disappointment, we have a silly, almost comical, wouldn't you agree, tiff.

Did Amelia and George have these kind of tiffs? Probably. What really goes on in the private day-to-day lives behind closed doors? I have always wondered about that when I drive by or fly over thousands of

100

houses, neighborhoods, people in cars. There are individuals in each having different yet perhaps similar encounters going on.

Amelia did think about that in the same way, as we can see from her writing on her takeoff and beginning of her solo Hawaiian flight. "My course lay over the edge of Honolulu. As I flew over that lovely city and realized it was just about the close of the business day, the thought flashed through my mind that everyone was going to supper – but me."

More amazing to her on this flight at this time, was that a local radio station put GP on to talk to her:

> Suddenly, I heard the music stop and the announcer's voice say, "We are interrupting our music program with an important news flash. Amelia Earhart has just taken off from Honolulu on an attempted flight to Oakland," Telling Me!

> Then I heard my husband's voice as if he were in the next room saying: "Amelia Earhart," so clear to me, sitting out there over the Pacific. It was really one of the high points of the flight.[13]

Gore Vidal talks about the Putnams having marital problems: "She was certainly sick of GP pushing her." But this is a serious situation. I'm wondering whether they had silly disagreements that melt away and result in what some people call "make-up sex afterward," not that we did. We just went to sleep and I woke up at 8:15 a.m.

Still concerned that my hubby would miss out on his beauty sleep, I figured out how to turn off the set alarm on his IPhone, which apparently had a Marimba alarm ring set, and felt successful about letting him sleep.

Ironically, Ned woke up briefly, I told him I turned off the alarm. "Thank you," he said, which made me smile and shake my head somewhat surprised. I kissed him on the forehead. "You silly boy," I softly responded, and back to sleep he went.

I would like to have been a fly on the wall to see if such little disagreements, small miscommunications, lighthearted arguments, occurred between the famous couple.

I'll have to read between the lines.

I love this letter because it shows that all families deal with trying to get along and further demonstrates how much Amelia wanted a good relationship with George's children. In this case his eldest son David and his new bride, Nilla.

George's letter postmarked March 11, 1934, to Nilla on a her possible visit:

> Dear Nilla,
> Don't buy much. Amelia and I would enjoy fitting you out
> . . . sort of a left handed wedding present. You can count on it.
> Please feel sure that you have two good friends here (George &
> Amelia) and that everything will be as easy as can be.

Amelia added her own personal handwritten note of encouragement to be a supportive stepmother and wife.

> "And I echo all that David's Dad has said."[14]

Dear Reader . . .

Looks to me like they enjoyed the journey, aviation and each other. What do you think?

How do you and your loved ones tend to resolve small quarrels?

CHAPTER SIX

ACTIVITIES

Not Just a Flyer by Any Means

ATHLETICS
Written September 2011

Early morning swim. Goal, one hundred laps. Yeah! I did like to have a goal, to conquer and complete it. Feels good, feels accomplished.

Amelia, I think, was of the same frame of mind.

Athletics were a frustration and a joy for her.

> Unfortunately I lived at a time when girls were still girls. Though reading was considered proper, many of my outdoor exercises were not. I was fond of basketball, bicycling, tennis and I tried any and all strenuous games. With no instruction in any sport, I wasn't good enough in myself to excel later. I wish that the vogue of teaching youngsters to learn correct form in athletics had been as universal then (early 1900s) as it is now (1930s). With the intense pleasure exercise gave me, I might have attained more skill and more grace than I did. As it was, I just played exultingly, and built up all kinds of wrong habits, a frustrated Amelia pronounced.[1]

"Like many middle western families, we trundled off to a lake and ours happened to be in (Worthington) Minnesota for the summer."[2] There Amelia learned to ride a pony on her own. She went on to become an accomplished rider.

Prophetically, while horseback riding with her sister Muriel in Toronto, an interesting connection to flying was observed by Captain Spaulding of the Royal Flying Corps. "Watching the way you ride that horse reminds me of the way I have to fly my plane," and he invited Amelia and Muriel to the corps airfield.

> Our physical abilities were encouraged by our mother. Not surprising, since mother was the first woman to climb the last mile of Pikes Peak. Mother made us the first gymnastic suits in town which we displayed on Saturdays much to the disdain

of the other properly skirted little girls. We felt very free and athletic.[3]

Notice Amelia said "we," referring to herself and sister Muriel. The freedom and daredevil attributes seem to have been assisted by her mother's encouragement. One daughter remained conventional and the other became a legend, fearless and adventuresome. The following is one of my favorite quotations and stories related by Amelia:

> Along with bloomers, coasting while lying flat on the sled was considered rough for girls. Such absurdities, when I looked back on them, make me seem incredibly old. However, that condemned tomboy method of sledding once saved my life. I was zipping down one of the really steep hills in town when a junk man's cart, pulled by a horse with enormous blinders, came out from a side road. The hill was so icy that I couldn't turn and the junk man didn't hear the squeals of warning. In a second my sled had slipped between the front and back legs of the horse and got clear, before either he or I knew what had happened. Had I been sitting up, either my head or the horse's ribs would have suffered contact-probably the horse's ribs.[4]

She even made her own clothes "to give ease of movement and simplicity."

Her grandmother was the most traditional and proper member of the family. "I know I worried my grandmother considerably by running home from school and jumping over the fence that surrounded our house," recollected Amelia. "When I was a small girl, said my grand mother, I did nothing more strenuous than roll my hoop in the public square." Amelia continued, "I felt very unladylike, and for the next succession of days, I walked around to the gate. Now probably, if I had been a boy, it would have been perfectly natural."[5]

Her grandfather, Judge Alfred Otis, seemed a bit at odds with this, having bought his grand daughter a hunting gun and another time a football, which might explain her mother's open attitude toward sports for the enjoyment of physical activities for herself and her daughters.

Or this most telling note:

> A Christmas letter to my father about this time began somewhat
> as follows: "Dear Dad, Muriel and I would like footballs this
> year, please. We need them specially, as we have plenty of
> baseballs, bats, etc." Christmas came and so did the footballs.[6]

Sisters Muriel and Amelia Earhart at play, 1906.

Amelia's frustration with female inequality shows up in all aspects of
her life, from the lack of "strong female heroines" with which to identify
in novels she read as a young girl to the acceptance of women as equally
capable pilots alongside men. "A pilot is a pilot," Amelia was filmed
saying at a White House press conference.

Dear Reader . . .

How were you raised: traditional, status quo or were you taught to try something new, go against convention?

How has that influenced your life, career, leisure, and child rearing?

How do you raise your children regarding trying new things, going against the set traditions small or large? Against gender-stereotyped behavior?

Share with Amelia and Me.

DID AMELIA MARY EARHART DANCE?

Written July 21, 2013

I'm going to my Sunday Ballet class.
I thought, "Did Amelia dance?"

Amelia wrote of her high school days, "I liked to dance, but no one asked me. I had a few faithfuls, but sat out most of the time, not for lack of interest."[7]

George Putnam also "looked passed me as if I were a sack of potatoes" upon their first meeting, and yet he later asked her to marry him six times before accepting.

Amelia "liked any and all sports." I think dance can be included in that. She was a physical person, limber, fearless and enthusiastic. Did she dance with royalty? She most definitely did.

June 1, 1932, the *Pittsburg Press* reported in an article by The United Press,

> LONDON, June 1 – The Prince of Wales danced with Amelia Earhart Putnam last night and found the American flier so skillful on her feet that he grumbled when they were forced to stop after fox-trot-ting through many numbers.

> Miss Earhart arrived at the Derby Ball at Grosvenor House shortly after the Prince appeared. She was wearing an apple green satin dress that made her appear even taller than she is – and she is taller than the Prince. She was taken to the Prince's table and he rose to greet her. The Prince gallantly offered his chair to Miss Earhart. She accepted and later the heir to the British throne asked Miss Earhart to dance. The orchestra was playing a fast fox-trot, "The Tiger Rag" and when it ended the Prince, grumbling told Miss Earhart, "We need more like that."

The orchestra leader seemed to get the idea, and the music began again. It was "The Tiger Rag" and the Prince promptly led Miss Earhart back for the fourth dance.

Amelia had arrived in London after becoming the first woman to fly solo across the Atlantic, landing her red Lockheed Vega 5B in a field near Londonderry, Ireland May 21, 1932, five years to the day after Lindbergh's crossings. Amelia was now the belle of the ball with no lack of dance requests.

DESIGNING CLOTHES

Written July 23, 2013

Restrictive clothing leads to restrictive lives. As Muriel will attest, I was always redesigning our clothes. Partly out of necessity due to Dad's battle with the bottle and to bring about ease of movement and simplicity. I used to design my own clothes. This was like the fire bell to the old fire horse. I was right there snorting.

Fame gave Amelia the opportunity to design her own clothing line. "In 1934 I found myself designing fashion, modeling and writing for fashion magazines."

"My clothes will be cut for comfort from my own designs. How I've suffered with sIeeves that were too short or shoulders too tight! I try to keep it in mind I want to make clothes that are well-cut for active living and working, smart and simple and inexpensive. The middle of the road all along. I don't want to do anything extreme in the way of gadgets. I use mostly tan, brown, blue and green for colors besides a lot of white but no very vivid or trying shades."[8]

Here we differ, as I enjoy summer colors of bright yellow, hot pink, and turquoise among others.

Dear Reader . . .

Would you have bought her clothes?

Would it be due to her name or the practical nature of the line?

What do you base your clothing choices on today?

Do you think it was the times that contributed to a more relaxed clothing style, or did Amelia influence this change?

DESIGNING CLOTHES

. . . Continued, Written July 23, 2013

I myself loved playing dress up as a child and still do. I enjoy putting outfits together. I find it fun and relaxing.

Late last night, not sleepy enough to go to bed, I dressed up in my never-before-worn olive green formal gown. I added the matching silver/green forearm gloves, light-catching silvery threaded green shawl, $100 dollar (did I really pay that!) plaited olive green ribboned clutch purse adorned with a rhinestone-enhanced clasp. Lots of green, but it looks great! I stepped into my gold and silver slightly platform heels. I pranced in a kind of wobbly tiptoe upstairs, to model my creations for my husband. It was 1:30 in the morning. It just wasn't any fun without an audience.

There he was on the computer. I cleared my throat, said "Hi" to get his attention. He in turn, without looking up at me, focused on his computer screen, said, "Here look at this."

I, in turn, tried to draw his attention to me again. I finally walked over, gently touched his shoulder and lightly kissed him on the cheek, saying, "Well what do you think?" He laughed, enjoying my visual surprise.

"I'll never get to wear this. No formal occasions," I pouted.

"How about to a premier?" he responded.

"Haven't been to any lately," I added.

"What about this one" he said, indicating and staring at a video on the iMac computer screen. I laughed. Then taking a second glance, realized it was a movie he had just completed of our trip to Washington D.C.!

My special event had arrived! "I love you," I said, giving him a gentle kiss and loving hug with my silky gloved forearm, laying my head atop his soft curly black hair. He smiled up at me, cheeks receiving the rise of a broad smile, "I love you," he replied.

Then I stepped out of my heels, removed my shawl, gloves and attended the premier of our first long awaited trip to Washington D.C.

"You did a beautiful job on this," complimenting him. And, "I was dressed for the occasion," I delightfully added.

ACTIVITIES: YOUR OWN

Written August 31, 2013

Here's mine: Ballet, five years old and it has been my safe place, my sanctuary always.

Thank you to my mother for taking me to ballet classes beginning at age five. She spent that money on me instead of herself and gave me the gift of educated dance.

I must have given her joy to do the things that she had somehow researched or felt were good for a child. I know she liked the Rockettes of New York. Also, she said that I was a "jumping jack" and she didn't know what to do with me, so she gave me dance.

It probably was a combination of things. Mostly, being a good mom and finding the answers to fulfilling the needs of her little "Birdie."

The author at age five in ballet class.

Dear Reader . . .

Are there activities you love that are your "safe place, your sanctuary"?

Are there activities you would like to try?

Are there any activities you have tried to do, but were not given the proper instruction as a young person, and felt you missed out?

Here's your space to create your lost dreams, make them a reality and remind yourself of the activities you love or would love to delve into again or anew.

Don't forget to add a photo of yourself doing something you worked at in all your joyfulness.

EATING

Written December 2011

If I eat late at night, I stay up late, and even then, I feel my stomach too heavy to fall asleep.

If I don't eat before bedtime, just hop in bed as soon as I am tired, even if a little hungry, and "daydream" about food, I will fall asleep comfortably, waking up to enjoy a good breakfast.

How did Amelia deal with food? She barely ate or drank anything during a flight. During her solo Atlantic flight, Amelia "sipped one can of tomato juice." My friend and fellow historian, Giacinta Bradley Koontz, suggested that this was calculated as to avoid the need to relieve herself, since facilities were not available. This is plausible.

Amelia did not seem to find food a major aspect or interest. She is quoted as saying upon completing a long flight, "I vanquished a whole chicken." However, after another long flight, she said, "I didn't eat for a long while even afterwards."

RELAXATION

Written December 2011

"What did Amelia do to relax?" I ask myself as I sit lounging on my pillow-laden throne, playing on my Facebook pages. Totally a waste of time, which made me wonder, did Amelia ever waste time doodling or just daydreaming?

I've seen photos of her sitting on the ground, legs crossed at the ankle, looking out, or on a boat with hubby enjoying the ocean breezes. She definitely appears to have savored just being alone in her airplane or at a residence.

We know she loved playing sports of all kinds in addition to gardening, writing poetry and letters to mom and sister Muriel, reading, and visiting friends. She must have had an artistic soul and seen the details as only an artistic mind can: the beauty, color, emotions of people, places and things. One can see these in her poetry, photography and clothing designs.

Amelia Earhart enjoyed flowers and gardening. Pictured above is her copper watering can.

I say this, for I discovered these elements myself when involved in painting. I then became aware of the details of flowers, the changing light, the movement of trees kissed by the wind.

On Amelia's Friendship flight, she wrote, "All I did was lie on my tummy and take pictures of clouds . . . Dawn touches them with rose that melts into gold. Evening colors them with a myriad of changing color till grey envelopes all."

Yes, I am sure Meile, a nickname acquired because her younger sister couldn't pronounce Amelia, did relax deep in thought, perhaps sitting on a rooftop, for which she was chastised at school, or when reading books and thinking there needed to be books about girls doing fantastic feats of courage.

> There are no heroines following the shining paths of romantic adventure, as do the heroes of boy's books. For instance, who ever heard of a girl – a pleasant one – shipping on a oil tanker, say, finding the crew about to mutiny and saving the captain's life (while quelling the mutiny) with a well disabling pistol shot at the leader of the gang! No, goings-on of this sort are left to the masculine characters, to be lived over joyously by the boy readers. Of course girls have been reading the so-called "boys books" ever since there were such. But consider what it means to do so. Instead of closing the covers with shining eyes and the happy thought, "That might happen to me someday!" turning the final page, can only sigh regretfully, "Oh, dear, that can never happen to me – because "I'm not a boy!" . . . Of

course before 'girl' books such as I have hinted at can be written, women must have accomplished enough to supply the material.[9]

A self-fulfilling wish as she became that heroine.

Amelia became that very legend of womanhood about which books are written. Amelia Earhart was and is a shining example of what any woman can accomplish by putting her mind to it.

> When asked later why she had flown the Atlantic solo Amelia replied: "I just wanted to see if I could fly the Atlantic alone. We all fly Atlantics in our own way. If someone does something against tradition, neighborhood opinion and so called "common sense" that is an Atlantic . . . I flew the Atlantic because I wanted to . . . To want in one's heart to do a thing, for its own sake; to enjoy doing it; to concentrate all one's energies upon it – that is not only the surest guarantee of its success, it is also being true to oneself."[10]

Dear Reader . . .

Do you stop amid your busy day's activities and take a moment to "smell the roses"?

What do you have in common with our friend Amelia as you relax?

By attempting new directions or goals, do you learn more about previous events in your life?

Name a few for fun. Be surprised.

A LITTLE MORE R & R

Written December 2011

I watch British shows. Did Amelia go to the movies, theatre, and museums? Amelia and George did host Hollywood royalty, who I am sure were also flattered to be in the presence of the most famous aviator and entertained at their home in Rye, New York. Amelia is seen posing with screen legends, Cary Grant, Douglas Fairbanks Sr., Mary Pickford, and many others. But I never read about them going to see a movie, a screening at the studios (which would allow for privacy) or an art exhibit.

Flying was originally a hobby for Amelia and where she found the most freedom and relaxation, "After midnight, the moon set, and I was alone with the stars. I have often said that the lure of flying is the lure of beauty."[11]

As noted, writing poetry gave her pleasure, and as a young woman, she did submit to magazines under the pen name, Emile A. Hart. She wrote for the 99s newsletter, even sending in an article an hour before one of her famous flights.

She did not ask others to fly with her, but waited for them to ask. George Palmer Putnam Jr. related to me personally that Amelia took him flying as a little boy, and she was "so nice."

Her hobbies and her goals seemed to intersect. What she enjoyed, she enjoyed to the fullest.

VACATIONS

Did Amelia Ever Go On Vacations?
Written March 9, 2012

She never took a honeymoon, but went straight back to work the day following her marriage to GP.

After her solo Atlantic flight in 1932, the cruise returning from France was probably for relaxation. She definitely wanted George to meet her in Paris and return on the ship with her to the USA as she "couldn't face the crowds alone."

She traveled from place to place as a child due to her father's job as a railroad attorney. But she and her sister spent summers at their grandparents' home in Atchison, Kansas, which was a haven of luxury and stability.

When Amelia was about thirteen, her family took their first vacation in Worthington, Minnesota, enjoying the lake as her father, Edwin, was now doing well. The following year all that changed when he became addicted to alcohol.[12]

In adulthood, Amelia's vacations always seemed tied in with work.

Although my family's income was very modest, as a child I always went on vacations to fun and interesting places by train, bus or car, creating memories that lasted a lifetime: Highland Springs, Disneyland, Las Vegas, Lake Tahoe, Palo Alto, Santa Barbara, and other California locals. I was always grateful and it makes me smile to this day.

In the early 1930s, Carl Dunrud purchased the Kirwin area and the lands around it. Six-and-a-half miles below Kirwin, he built the Double D. Dude Ranch. Among his first guests were Amelia Earhart and her husband, George Putnam. Later, Earhart asked Dunrud to build a cabin for her, where she planned to come after her around-the-world flight in 1937. When she disappeared on that flight, the cabin was four logs high and construction stopped. The cabin was never finished. It can be seen by hiking about one mile past Kirwin, Wyoming.

If Amelia didn't take time off during her nine-year flying career, it definitely looks like she and George were planning to enjoy life away from the spotlight of fame in the hinterlands of Wyoming after her round-the-world flight.

The plans for building this cabin and the remodeling of their home to include a residence for her mother Amy, in Toluca Lake, California demonstrate for me that Amelia was looking forward to a beautiful future with her husband and mother.

Rumors of a failing marriage, her desire to disappear on her last flight only to return incognito, seem extremely far-fetched and without basis. At least that is the opinion of this researcher.

Amelia, Muriel, their father, Edwin and the porter, Tomiko, on the end of a railroad car. 1911 or 1912 Atchison, Kansas.

Dear Reader . . .

What is your personal take?
Did Amelia vacation apart from work? Let me know if you find she did.

What is your vacation history? Are you a workaholic? Are your
vacations tied with your work? Is that more satisfying?

OR do you like to vacation for adventure, follow an interest or hobby or
just stop and relax from your daily routine?

What is your dream vacation? Is it a romantic weekend away,
snow camping, people watching or going to study art in Florence, Italy?

CHAPTER SEVEN
PERSPECTIVES AND FLIGHT

AMELIA'S THOUGHTS ON CHILDREN, PREGNANCY

"There's another little person."
Written August 5, 2013

Tonight at 7:40 p.m. on the G-chat, with Ned, Peter, Eli, and me, our daughter told us, "We're expecting a baby."

For the first time in my life I was speechless! Really.

I didn't, couldn't say anything. I was sooo surprised. I had worked at putting it out of my mind. If she decided at some point, I thought that would be in the future. Maybe five or ten years since she had her new job and Peter, her husband, had just started a business.

She said that there is never a good time, "It's now or never," and that she didn't want to be thirty-five or older. So, she said they decided to try, and she immediately got pregnant seven and a half weeks ago!

I am thrilled and speechless, surprised and happy. I think Ned, my husband, is too, but he shows little emotion, except if he is annoyed. Even with this announcement when I started talking about it, he changed the subject to have me leave the room by suggesting, "Isn't your show on?"

Since he is retired, maybe because he is home all the time, one thinks there is someone to talk with and share with. It is just more time at home with less spoken or what seems like less.

That being said, we were delighted and happy, and I prayed for the best. For both my children.

Where does Amelia come in on all this? What were her thoughts on children, on pregnancy?

There is speculation that she was pregnant during her last flight. Elgen Long, author of *The Mystery Solved*, speculates this, as do others because she was sick in the mornings on her round-the-world flight.

Amelia had strong feelings about children and birth control. For a wedding gift, she gave her sister Muriel *The Drs. Manuel of Marriage*, a book on birth control.

On the other hand, she enjoyed teaching immigrant children at Dennison House in Boston, a job to which she expected to continue after her initial fight across the Atlantic. In addition, she was well liked by her stepchildren, David and George Jr. She just thought having a child "takes too long."

Dear Reader . . .

Where do you think Amelia stood on the issue of children?

Where do you stand on the issue of children?

Do you think women can have a high profile career, marriage and children successfully?

What is your personal experience?

PLANS SET IN MOTION

Written March 21, 2012

One of my dance instructors said, "At year's end, start being where you want to be." In this way, you are going into the New Year with momentum, already on your way to achieving the goal or results you desire instead of proposing a New Year's resolution.

Amelia may not have made her decision to prepare for her round-the-world flight on or before a new year began, but she did have a definite decision-making moment when her focus and plan to circumnavigate the globe at the equator crystallized.

That was on her non-stop flight from Mexico City to New York in May of 1935. On all previous flights she had a layer of clouds beneath her trusty red Vega, which apparently gave her the illusion of safety. On this flight, with clear skies and good visibility, she only saw huge expanses of ocean below.

It occurred to Amelia that if her single engine Vega failed, there was no backup. It was then that Amelia decided she would fly only two engine planes. That was the beginning of the formation of her plan for her longest, most expensive adventure, and the adaptation of the flying laboratory, the Lockheed Electra.

Photo: RED VEGA now at the Smithsonian in Washington DC.

The author at the Smithsonian in front of Amelia's Red Vega.

Amelia Earhart in front of the Lockheed Electra

Dear Reader . . .

What would you like to start on at the end of the year to get going into the New Year?

FEELING WORTHY OF THE ACCOLADES

Written November 2011

Today I heard in my head a familiar quote and a familiar feeling but did not put them together.

Since the Clint Eastwood directed biopic *J. Edgar* has been promoted, everyone has been "gaga" about my appearance in the film.

I was very glad to be hired, working and, thank goodness, not cut.

I would remind anyone who mentioned my role in the film, that I have done significant roles, for major directors and producers, even an Emmy winning movie-of-the-week, but to no avail. The idea that I did this role remained, in their mind, my most significant credit.

For example, the first comment came when I was a guest speaker at a performing arts high school. The instructor said, "This is the biggest thing you've ever done." I was surprised and answered, "No, it is just current."

I could not put together the accolades for this role in *J. Edgar* with my "don't blink or you will miss me" role and the lack of recognition for some of my really outstanding film work.

But now, through talking with my son, I understand the excitement by friends, old and new, over my good fortune to be in *J. Edgar*. I am accepting, even enjoying their over-the-top reactions.

My son, Daryl, pointed out that Clint Eastwood is an icon. He is the director of our time. I realized that one little scene afforded me the opportunity to actually work alongside him and interact with him and his star Leonardo DiCaprio.

This morning it hit me. I truly understood Amelia Earhart's drive and determination to complete a solo Atlantic Flight in 1932, four years after her 1928 Friendship flight crossing the Atlantic as the first female passenger in history. Amelia was the toast of the town, the heroine of the flight. She kept telling the press, "But it's the boys, they did all the flying." Pilots Wilmer Stultz and Louis Gordon, who actually flew the Friendship with Amelia as the passenger, were ignored by the press

"Someday I will have to do it alone, if only to vindicate myself. I'm a false heroine and that makes me feel very guilty. Someday I will redeem my self respect, I can't live without it."[1]

When I remembered Amelia's quotation, I realized that was the moment she started to plan her solo Atlantic flight, and I knew I needed to plan

1928 The *Friendship* crew is greeted upon completing their Atlantic crossing. L to R: Amy Guest, Louis E. Gordon, Amelia Earhart, Wilmer Stultz, Mrs. Foster Welch (Southampton, England)

my own film with a role "to vindicate myself" and feel worthy of the accolades.

Apparently, we both functioned on guilt as a motivator for better or worse.

Dear Reader . . .

Do you function on guilt?

What motivates you to change your course or initiate a new goal?

Do you think guilt is a poor excuse for motivation?

Is it good to be motivated by anything, as long as the goal is worthwhile? Share with us, dear reader.

LONELY versus ALONE

Written August 26, 2011

When feeling alone, lonely and sad about being alone, I remembered how Amelia loved flying because she could be alone in the clouds.

Today, here I type on an iPad, use satellite phones to communicate the world over in less than a second and am flying to Seattle next month, Scandinavia next year. I've been to Israel, Europe. The first time I traveled to Europe, I went alone, I loved it and I learned so much about myself . . . fond memories. Alone isn't necessarily lonely.

I guess loneliness is relative. It depends on one's point of view. I'll admit it was always a little unsettling at the beginning, arriving in each new place by myself, but after summoning up a little bravery and leaving my hotel room, it was fun, interesting and exciting to "adventure about." As Amelia would say, "Adventure is worthwhile in itself."

Also, regarding Amelia's alone time, a journalist remarked and Amelia commented, "The news can be somewhat cruel at times, regarding my hair and the state it is in." It was written . . . "in the long lonely stretches over the calm and blue Pacific, Comb your hair kid, comb your hair."[2]

SPIRITUALITY and BHUTAN

Written January 1, 2012

I was watching a television show about the country of Bhutan.

The Bhutanese are Buddhist. The leadership philosophy of the country is based on "happiness of mind." The goal is to "live in the middle." Social, environmental, family values, balance of leisure and work, quality of physical environment, lead to happiness.

Taking the middle path to happiness, "Gross National Happiness" is a metric created by King Jigmi of Bhutan, enlightened philosopher king. According to the king, once you have reached a certain amount of money, then having more will not make you any happier.

Did Amelia find this balance for happiness? Was she happy?

Her financial worries ended due to her celebrity, making her financially secure through the sale of her books, lecture tours and product endorsements. She could give financial support to her mother Amy, sister Muriel and other family members and friends, which she did generously. She obviously felt a sense of satisfaction to be able to do so. The smart marketing of her publisher-husband made them a successful team and wealthier beyond "the middle." However, Amelia had her own money to use as she saw fit.

We know that Amelia discovered herself to be "happier than I ever imagined" once marrying George Palmer Putman, as we read in the letter to her mother at the beginning of her marriage.

We have seen that she gained great joy from physical activities of sports, the natural environment and was passionate about her flying career. She definitely appears to have fulfilled the "happiness of mind."

King Jigmi does not include spirituality in his "Gross National Happiness" for as a Buddhist country, perhaps that is a given. As for

148

Amelia, raised as an Episcopalian, she did have a spiritual philosophy of her own:

> Amelia wrote, "I think of God as symbol for good – thinking good, identifying good in everybody and everything. This God I think of is not an abstraction, but a vitalizing, universal force, eternally present, and at all times available."[3]

Gives us much to ponder, gives us pause.

Dear Reader . . .

What are your thoughts? Do you have a balanced life?

Do you feel that Amelia did feel happy?

Are you happy? Or are there elements missing that would round out your life?

And if so, how can you incorporate those elements into your life?

AMELIA EARHART AND SEXUALITY

Was Amelia a sexual person?
Written February 2, 2012

From the letter to George on their wedding day, which may have been the first prenuptial agreement, she writes:

> I shall not hold you to any medieval code of faithfulness to me nor shall I consider myself bound to you similarly. If we can be honest I think the difficulties which arise may best be avoided should you or I become interested deeply or in passing in anyone else.[4]

She was mentioned in the 1935 divorce allegations of Paul Mantz, her technical advisor, as "the other woman." There has always been a question as to whether she was not only with other men, but also with other women. I find no evidence in her writings other than as friend and professional colleague in either case.

Eugene Vidal carried a picture of Amelia in his pocket watch, which his son, Gore, felt indicated an intimate relationship between Amelia and his father. Was there ever a tryst between Eugene Vidal and Amelia? Did George know? Was Gore Vidal correct? So far there is only speculation and much room for discussion.

Amelia was shy in public, not comfortable displaying affection, but at home with George, according to her step granddaughter, Sally Putnam Chapman, "Privately they were an affectionate couple, touching and holding hands" on the way to the airport before her round-the-world-flight.[5]

We know marriage was not in Amelia's plans. She refused GP's many proposals and told the press when asked, "I'll marry sometime in the next fifty years," but she finally decided to agree. It appears she was happy she made the decision. They appeared to have built a good life together.

Dear Reader . . .

What are your thoughts, my Dear Readers?

Do you think Amelia was loyal to George or that she took lovers?

Do you think Amelia loved George?

How do you think Amelia came up with the idea of her prenuptial letter?

Do you think it was a good idea? Share your thoughts.

Chapter Eight
PERSONALITY

DECISIONS

"Worry retards reaction and makes clear-cut decisions impossible."
(Amelia Earhart)
Written Oct 16, 2011

On Amelia's preparation for her solo Atlantic flight, George Palmer Putnam was the one who could not sleep nights, but Amelia did. She told her neighbor Ruth Nichols, who was also preparing to fly the Atlantic, that one had to take chances on long distance flights, "So I don't bother to go into all the possible accidents that might happen. I just don't think about crackups."

> The time to worry is three months before a flight, Amelia declared. Decide then whether or not the goal is worth the risks involved. If it is, stop worrying. To worry is to add another hazard. It retards reactions, makes one unfit. Hamlet would have been a bad aviator. He worried too much.[1]

> George Palmer Putnam added, "I do know that always, where her flying brought cause for fear, I was the frightened one."[2]

Amelia's outlook occurred to me as I contemplated my return trip to L.A. from Seattle. I started to be concerned about the flight. I started to feel bad that I wasn't staying one more night since my son-in-law was coming home a day later than I had thought. If I stayed, I would have one more day to learn about and be with my little grandson, seeing him at his daycare or just walking around Seattle by myself, as my daughter was going to work the next day.

Then I remembered Amelia's point of view and the philosophy I had subscribed to as a young girl: "No Regrets." This was my mantra from the age of fifteen when I heard my mother on the telephone learning of the death of her most admired sister, Estelle. Mother deeply regretted not having visited Estelle back in Chicago since moving to California when pregnant with me. I vowed at that time that I would always do everything I wanted to do as long as it did not hurt someone else, and I have done just that.

156

I still do the things I really want to do, but in recent years, I find myself regretting, second-guessing or questioning some of my choices or decisions.

Amelia's point of view:

> The most difficult thing is the decision to act. The rest is merely tenacity. The fears are paper tigers. You can do anything you decide to do. You can act to change and control your life and the procedure. The process is its own reward.[3]

Hopefully, adopting Amelia's strength of decision-making and ability to let go of worry about possible mishaps or refusal to give in to regret, will be freeing.

Dear Reader . . .

Are you a worrier like me?

Do you make decisions and then look back thinking, "If only I had done such and such?"

Or are you like Amelia, making a decision and letting go, no longer questioning your decision?

VULNERABILITIES

Written February 2, 2012

Was Amelia always a pillar of strength for family, friends and the world of aviation? Was she always self assured, never in need of others?

For the most part, the answer is yes. But in this letter to her mom, we get a glimpse that even the most adventurous and fearless have their needs, fears and vulnerabilities.

New York, Nov. 4, 1932

Dear Mother,
I just returned from Chicago and points west where I have had one of the first of my lectures. Everything went well. I flew and trained when necessary and did not attempt to go so far by car.

I shall be here ten days and then start out in New England. GP is going with me to the most northern points as I do not like the territory very well as you know and need moral support.[4]

Amelia may have been fearless and adventuresome, but she was not by nature a public person, and thus needed the support, protection and strength of GP at times – and she was willing to ask for it, which was part of her charm. A slight vulnerability and shyness, much reminiscent of the late Princess Diane of England comes to mind.

Both were women from opposite social and economic strata, beloved by the public like no others; both were naturally shy and uncomfortable with fame and public attention, but they learned to use the spotlight for improving the lot of others since seclusion was not an option for either one of them.

GETTING THINGS DONE

Written August 8, 2013

I am trying to get a personal appointment, get a window treatment ordered, confirm a ticket purchase. I am encountering frustration at the lack of efficiency in response to my emails, purchases, people not reading my emails, or not listening to phone messages. I am frustrated by the inability to get someone on the phone after that person had confirmed that they would be waiting for my call to finalize an order at a specific time.

Did Amelia feel as frustrated when ordering plane parts, building her house in Toluca Lake, encountering contractors, dealing with slow and inefficient responses to her inquiries which then required constant pressure in order to get things done?

I am sure she did. For example, on her round-the-world flight, her first attempt resulted in a crash, which delayed the flight by two months. That in itself is an amazingly short time to repair, re-route, reschedule, and totally reorganize the flight.

Not only did they need financing amounting to $50,000 for repairs to the Lockheed Electra (quite a sum in those days), but also her flight companions could not continue on the new flight. Paul Mantz, her technical advisor bowed out; it was said due to conflicts with George Putnam, who was now left in charge and knew nothing of airplanes. Harry Manning, her expert radio man had other commitments. This left only Fred Noonan, a top navigator formerly with Pan Am, but who lacked knowledge of radio operations, as did Amelia and GP. As navigator Brad Washburn said, "This was the Putnams' downfall. They needed to know a lot about radio."

So whereas my frustration is about minor things, on Amelia's last flight, her frustration must have been overwhelming. Maybe that is why the Putnams did so much themselves – to make sure things would get done. Amelia always multitasked.

AMELIA: MONEY MATTERS

Written July 8, 2013

I am thinking of applying once again for unemployment benefits. I should be eligible . . . again. Geez . . . The life of an actor. When I applied the first time, the clerk at the Employment Development Office, upon hearing I was an actor, replied smilingly, "You'll be here often."

At the time I naively smiled with a pleasant chuckle and thought, "How cutely funny." Boy was he right!

How did Amelia make her living? How did she get paid, make ends meet before fame and during the height of her celebrity?

Amelia was a pragmatist when it came to finances, which stands in stark contrast to the adrenaline-fueled dare-devilish exploits for which she is so well known. Early on, Amelia recognized the lack of control demonstrated by her immediate family with regard to finances. In a letter to her mother she writes, "Our family has never been good at money matters." To that end, Amelia was always attaching stipulations when giving money to her sister Muriel or her mother Amy, which, once a famous aviator, she did generously and often.

Dear Mother,   Rye, Fall of 1931

     I am enclosing a check for $33. This plus $17 I sent last month makes $50. I am depositing the rest of the amount to your credit here. I am very much displeased at the use you have put what I hoped you would save. I am not working to help Albert (Amelia's brother-in-law) nor Pidge (her sister Muriel) much as I care for her. If they had not had that money perhaps they would have found means to economize before.

     I do not mean to be harsh, but I know the family failing about money. As for your paying board, such a thing is unthinkable as you have done all the housekeeping which more than compensates.

     It is true that I have a home and food but what I send yu (Amelia's shorthand for you) is what I myself earn and it does not come from GP. I feel the church gets some of what should go to living expenses and I have no wish to continue that to Pidge's loss . . .

Yr. Doter

A[5]

Amelia came from a well to do family, headed by the honorable Judge Alfred Otis, who had traveled by overland stage and flatboat up the Missouri River, establishing and prospering in Atchison, Kansas. Their elegant house overlooking the Missouri River is a walk back in history, and remains practically untouched to this day. Amelia's childhood was divided between living in the upscale household of her maternal grandparents and the struggling unstable home of her parents. As noted earlier, she attended sixteen different schools, graduating from Hyde Park High in Chicago.

As Amelia said, "Having lived a para-pathetic [sic] life, never long in one place for any length of time, I think photographs mean more to me than most people. They keep records fresh and memories strong." Photography was not only a hobby, but also a source of income. As Earhart put it, "I took on a series of jobs: telephone company. . . I liked the job and the boys, truck driver for a sand and gravel company, social worker, photographer, to pay for the (flying) lessons I so dearly wanted."[6]

Even at age seventeen, attending Ognotz School, she writes her mother, "I hate to spend money for things I never will need or want," regarding buying a barely used pair of patent leather shoes from a friend.[7]

After her sudden ascent to fame Amelia writes:

I went from earning just enough today for my lessons, to accumulating fifty thousand dollars from various avenues of work. This involved, twenty-seven lectures a month, eight articles a year for Cosmopolitan and promotions.[8]

Amelia was very focused on balancing her monetary resources, big or small, rich or poor, for what she deemed of importance to her.

Author Roberta Bassin seated in front of Amelia Earhart's ancestral home in Atchison, Kansas.

Dear Reader . . .

What do you think of the strong control Amelia exerted over monies she gave to her family?

Should money be gifted to others "with strings attached"?

How does Amelia's manner of using her funds compare with your own?

Do you spend money on impulse buying or do you spend on targeted purchases?

Or a little of both like me?

HAPPINESS DEMANDS AN EXCITING LIFE

Written December, 2011

It is my understanding, according to a Doris Rich interview, "Amelia had to have an exciting life."

I think I too feel I *have to have* different and interesting happenings going on to make life whole and complete. But they have to be connected to goals that I am working towards. I don't feel good – in fact, I feel downright anxious – when I don't have activities which are meaningful, fun and fulfilling. I do volunteer teaching at the Screen Actors Guild Conservatory because I need to feel worthwhile, to share my knowledge, to see young people excel. If I can help them achieve their dreams, that makes me happy.

That feeling of joy – happiness – isn't that what we all desire?

What motivated Amelia? Was it joy, happiness, adventure, a quest for quiet isolation, helping friends and family? Was it being able to share her knowledge, money, time, energy, opinions and style?

Resounding "YES" to all the above, as shown through her letters, books and poetry written throughout her life starting from an early age.

I related the story of Amelia at age seven, belly flopping on a sled downhill, passing right between the legs of a passing horse and jumping up triumphantly!

Her cousin, Ernest F. Tonsing, tells of the neighbors in Atchison, Kansas nervously watching Amelia babysitting her cousins, as she ran pushing the stroller so fast they feared the baby would be flung out. Amelia obviously found great joy in speed and adventure.

As a child, Amelia's imagination took her to far and exotic places. As an adult, "flying brought far places closer. The horizon and what lay beyond gained added lure," as Amelia said, following her desire for adventure and travel.[9]

Dear Reader . . .

What motivates you?

What fulfills and excites you?

Do you need excitement in your life? Or just the opposite?

CAUTION: WARY OF STRANGERS

Written July 13, 2013

At home, the doorbell rings. Police instruct home owners to never open the door. Be wary, don't answer. My son, a big guy, age thirty-eight (at the time), tiptoes past the door signaling to me with finger over lip . . . quiet. Time 11:30 a.m.

Yes, it is a beautiful July morning, but we are in caution mode. I glance out the window and see a white pickup truck with lawn mowers in it. Through the peephole, I cannot tell who it is. It must be a gardener at the wrong house. Our gardener comes on Wednesday. This is Saturday.

Finally, after numerous silent signals, my son asks, "Should I go outside?" I give him the okay.

The humble, very clean, nicely dressed man, in a long-sleeved evergreen shirt, khaki pants and large straw hat, speaking only Spanish, tries to explain his purpose.

My son, Daryl picks up the word "ficus" and realizes this man is here to trim our leafy ficus benjamina tree!

I employ my seven years of public school Spanish. After coercing my husband to enter the conversation, we immediately learn that the gardener is the father of our regular gardener and familiar to my husband.

All the kind man wanted was to trim the tree, as he couldn't do it on his regular day, which was "miercoles" (Wednesday)!!!!

Was Amelia Earhart – fearless, daredevil (by her own description), flier over oceans, mountains, driver alone across the country, defender of human rights – ever wary of the simple encounter, encroachment or approach of strangers?

YES, YES, YES! She became ever more cautious and unapproachable as her fame increased, exemplified previously in her letters dealing with promotional travel.

CHAPTER NINE
GOALS

GOALS: ORGANIC

Written May 24, 2013

Amelia, on the night of her first flight experience, told her family that evening at dinner, "I think I'd like to fly," but inwardly she thought, "I'd die if I didn't."[1]

As noted in chapter one, Amelia had been at an air show in Long Beach with her father. There she paid five dollars to take her first plane ride with pilot Frank Hawks. "By the time I had got two or three hundred feet off the ground, I knew I had to fly," she recalled. She was twenty-three.

This is a perfect example of the immediate organic birth of a passionate goal. Unplanned, an interest never experienced before but now an obsessive need to be accomplished, takes hold of an individual. Thus, flying became everything – and nothing would get in her way.

Amelia paid for the lessons herself by taking a job at the telephone company. She took a street car and then walked three miles each way to the Kinner airfield to take lessons from another female, Neta Snook, paying a dollar a minute, wearing riding breeches (jodhpurs) and greasing them up to fit in with the look of a flier.

I am searching for my goal, to feel passionate about it. That made me think of how Amelia's goal came about. She didn't sit down and think, "What goal should I set for myself?" She encountered her goal on that day, December 28, 1920, and became hooked on flying. I hope we all have that spontaneous lead into passion and follow our dreams.

Do I have a passionate need to write this book or any book on Amelia Mary Earhart? Am I creating a need? I do have a fear of not having written a book about her. I have all the knowledge, more than any other historical topic I have studied. I ask these questions of myself. I must acknowledge the obvious answer. Yes.

Dear Reader . . .

What is your passion?

What do you feel you need to do in order to feel complete?

Do you feel you have an expertise from which others would benefit and which you are driven to pursue more extensively to share with others?

Tell us about it.

TO PREPARE OR NOT TO PREPARE PROPERLY? THAT IS THE QUESTION.

Written November 6, 2013 9:15 a.m.

"One good flight left in me," quoted Amelia Earhart.
I could relate. I thought at the time, one last *Amelia Earhart: In Her Own Words* show left in me. Her Swan Song. My Swan Song.

Sunday I do a small show for a retirement and assisted living residence, Belmont Village in Burbank, California. Although I will probably continue to perform the show, my 99s banquet performance really felt like a culmination. I did it in a fabulous place, got a standing ovation and finally had a professional taping of it. I felt satisfied and complete.

My next goal was and is to complete this book and publish it.

The show does satisfy my need to perform as an actor, receive validation, share knowledge and motivate others. The Belmont show *is* perfect right now as it's been a while since I have booked a paying gig. This is a positive outlet for me. It also gets me going on my new goal of writing again and completing the next step for my Amelia Earhart book.

There, I feel better already. And I do have a commercial audition this morning. Yeahhhh!

Now for some breakfast. Ahhh breakfast, oatmeal, blueberries, tea, crackers. I'm feeling like a whole new person.

I have that commercial audition. Should I print out a copy beforehand? Thinking I "wasn't preparing properly" this morning. I must not do that.

This is what writer Doris Rich said of Amelia regarding her last flight. "She didn't prepare properly. She needed time and luck."[2] She had neither – and look what happened.

Dear Reader . . .

What is your swan song?

Have you completed one challenge so that you feel satisfied and ready to move onto the next?

Do you ever tackle an opportunity unprepared? How do you feel afterward?

Share your thoughts.

WHAT AMELIA WANTED

Children or Not?
Written August 23, 2011

Having a family was one of my natural priorities. I have been blessed with two children, but I remember as a little girl thinking that four children would make the perfect family. When our two children were pre-teens, sitting on my couch, I pictured a little one trying to walk holding onto the sofa and said to my husband, "Don't you miss having a little one around? The first two turned out so good, wouldn't you like two more?" His answer, "Why?"

Amelia would probably have agreed with him. Children were obviously not part of her plans, and she was not shy about discussing her strong attitude regarding birth control or child care with her sister Muriel and mother Amy as noted in private letters.

NAVIGATING HER CAREER:
THE ROOSEVELTS AND THE PRESS

Written August 23, 2011

Amelia was definite, strong willed and knew what the pressure points were to achieve desired results both privately and professionally.

She, like her husband, could be charming and strong, wise and opinionated, but unlike him, she was exceedingly likable and knew or learned how to navigate the politics of fame.

An excellent example is in her letter that I briefly alluded to in chapter one, to Amy regarding talking to the press while on European holiday:

(Undated & unsigned p.198 "Letters from Amelia")

Please don't down The Roosevelt Administration. It's all right to be reactionary inside but it is out of step with the times to sound off about the chosen people who have inherited or grabbed the earth. You must think of me when you converse and I believe the experiments carried on today point the way to a new social order when governments will be the voice of the proletariat far more than democracy ever can be.

In all cases be careful of reporters. They may find you out. Be cheerful with them and smile for photographs. The serious face in real life looks sour in print. The grinning face moderately pleasant. Don't express international opinions. Say you're on a quiet visit. You hope to fly across some time. You're going to probe around: not social visit. You approve of my flying: you don't know my plans for future: mention any special things which have impressed you.

(In England talk of English things, France French, Don't praise Westminster in Paris.) Look on cheerful side never tell of mishaps, lost baggage, cold mutton chops, runs in your hose, etc.

Amelia Earhart and First Lady Eleanor Roosevelt on a short flight to and from Baltimore.
Aviator Amelia Earhart points out the White House to resident First Lady Eleanor Roosevelt.
Location: Above Washington, DC, USA.

Amelia's relationship with Eleanor and Franklin D. Roosevelt was indeed a friendship. The two women, both worldwide celebrities extraordinaire, shared the love of flight. Amelia, in formal gown and long white gloves, took Eleanor for an airplane ride during a presidential gala!

Speculation abounds, due to the close ties, that Amelia's disappearance on her last flight in 1937 over the Pacific and subsequent "most extensive search for a private plane in history of flight," was crafted by Franklin Delano Roosevelt and Earhart to learn more about the Japanese military threat. There has never been a shred of evidence to support this theory or other speculations such as her being captured by the Japanese and taken to the island of Saipan, or landing on a coral reef on Nikumaroro Island . . . Well, let's talk about the other theories in another chapter or book or someone else's book. There are soooo many, many theories – and books for that matter!

PHYSICAL PAIN AND
FINAL LEG FROM LAE NEW GUINEA

Written December 21, 2011

I am in pain . . . joints, stomach, tired muscles ache . . . as I get up from a little rest after grocery shopping. Every move caused an "ooh, ache, ouch." I recalled that Amelia flew the last leg of her round-the-world flight feeling a million times worse than if she had a possible flu bug or suffered aches and pains from too much exercise.

Mind over matter – does it work? Does it work for you?

Amelia sure seemed to prove it to be the case. A bad back, severe sinus condition for which she was operated on many times, and a weak stomach did not prevent her from following her passion of flying the longest distances in confined cockpits, icy conditions, or sick to her stomach reactions.

When Amelia left Lae, New Guinea, she had been flying for forty-two days, on five hours of sleep a night. She was emaciated, had diarrhea, was rail thin, but also so hopeful that if she could make it to Howland Island, all would be well. Then on to Oakland to celebrate her last and final stunt. "I feel I have but one flight left in me," Amelia wrote.

"*Push through.*" I find myself writing those words almost resentfully. We're always pushing through. Hurrying on our long way, trying to get to some other place instead of enjoying the place we'd already got to. A situation, alas, about which there was no use complaining. After all this is not a voyage of sight-seeing. Only there were so many sights I wanted to see.[3]

Not much more than a month ago, I was on the shore of the Pacific looking westward. This evening, I looked eastward over the Pacific. In those fast-moving days which have intervened, the whole width of the world has passed behind us – except the broad ocean. I shall be glad when we have the hazards of its navigation behind us.[4]

Amelia Earhart disappeared over the Pacific three weeks shy of her fortieth birthday. She was a woman with a weak constitution but a strong determination.

Gee, I don't feel any pain, it has melted away, as hers must have when the quest becomes the endorphin of the body and mind.

Amelia was happiest and at peace alone, flying above the clouds as I discussed previously. The last takeoff from Lae must have seemed a natural, maybe peaceful leg in that she may have liked the idea that her navigator, Fred Noonan, may not have been up to his job, and that she would essentially be the solo pilot soaring into the blinding sunrise for 22 hours.

I hypothesize that she rather relished the idea of being, for all practical purposes, alone up there, completely in control, all quiet, doing what she liked best, never second-guessing or feeling fearful or regretful of her decisions, something I must incorporate into my daily life as well.

Amelia most probably died as she wished, "When I go, I'd like to in my plane. Quickly."[5]

PASSION

Written February 7, 2012

Passion for what one does is a painful loss when it disappears. Without it, one cannot feel motivated. Life stands still.

When I had lost my passion, my drive, I wanted it back, even if it meant frustration. For even frustration breeds creativity. Doing something in an area about which you are passionate, eventually succeeding and feeling personally fulfilled, that is success. That is happiness. Happiness is what you define it to be.

Do what you love, love what you do, and you will be happy, radiating joy and enthusiasm. Consequently, others will be touched by your "shining light" and reflect the brilliance back to the original source.

Amelia had this "shining light" and more.

Dear Reader . . .

Are desire and passion necessary to achieve one's goal?

What are your goals?

Are you motivated to achieve these goals by desire and passion?

DID AMELIA NEED TO LEAD
AN EXCITING LIFE?

Written July 25, 2013

If by exciting one means leading a life that is filled with variety, doing new things, "mixing it up," I find it to be a resounding "YES."

Why? How did I arrive at that conclusion?

This morning I did a lot of rearranging to go to two new groups or happenings. Nothing strange but new, both related to my acting passion: a new film school, which I briefly joined, was doing photo shoots, and a Women In Film actor's cold reading group was meeting. I hadn't attended either event before. I realized that it took some juggling to make the schedule work so I could go from one to the other. Both were in downtown Los Angeles, and I did not want to drive back and forth from the San Fernando Valley.

Getting out of my morning bath, I thought, "I don't want to be home tonight doing the same thing, watching the same show even though I had enjoyed it before and was a fan. I need to mix it up." It wasn't only for the career, but I apparently like doing career related events.

It was at that moment that I remembered what Doris Rich, author of *A Biography: Amelia Earhart*, said: Amelia Earhart "had to have an exciting life." Amelia's cousin, in remembrance said, "Amelia found herself easily bored," possibly leading to her being a master multitasker. Her lack of focus on her last flight has caused much debate. I, like most women, find myself multi tasking and juggling all the time.

I now recall that I have often thought Amelia and I both *had* to have excitement in our lives. I feel happy looking forward to doing something new, meeting new people, even figuring out a new schedule. As a consequence, my energy, mood, adrenaline rose.

Once again, as I worked on my play about Amelia, I am reminded that we both needed variety, excitement in our lives which were productive and goal oriented.

Dear Reader . . .

What do you do to mix things up, to make your life interesting and exciting?

Do you find the ordinary can be extraordinary?

Share your thoughts.

OVERWHELMED

Written July 22, 2013

I'm on the verge of tears when I think of all the things in my mind I want to do and accomplish.

My son's answer: "Just do a little at a time. Ten minutes."

Dallas, my career coach, sent an email blast from an author to just do five minutes at a time towards completing a task. My son, my coach, and now I myself, can see it works. Getting a little done at a time adds up, where as not doing anything but thinking about it, well you know, doesn't get you anywhere except unhappily frustrated and unfulfilled.

For a long time I was stuck because I didn't formulate my goals and couldn't move forward.

Now I *have* formulated my goals. (I wonder if it is due in part to taking Dallas Travers' class.) It is probably why I took the class because I was stuck. Now I am unstuck but overwhelmed with how to get it all done. It takes courage to move forward, as Amelia's poem "Courage" so aptly tells us. Answer . . . just do a little at a time. I am writing this to sort out my thoughts.

Amelia's poem, "Courage," written while still a social worker in Boston at Dennison House before she ever dreamed of becoming a famous aviatrix, always centers me and reminds me to take those "quantum leaps." Be brave, know and be reminded that life would be pretty boring if I were not "courageous" about doing what I need to do to attain my goals, gaining "peace" for following my passion and dreams and taking the steps to accomplish my goals one by one.

I now feel focused, renewed and confidently motivated.

Dear Reader . . .

Let's now focus on you.

Do you have a project that you keep putting off because just the thought of it is overwhelming? Something as simple as cleaning or organizing a closet can be such a task. Write it down.

Only do ten minutes of your overwhelming project. Share your results with us.

Pleasant surprise, I'll bet. Feels good to do a few minutes each day or every other day – and lo and behold – you've accomplished your goal!

PERFECTIONISM VERSUS PROFESSIONALISM

Written July 31, 2013

Another quagmire in which I feel overwhelmed: What do I need to do to get my acting career going?

I keep working on my craft. Originally I wanted to be the best actress I could be, and I did that. I did get jobs, but now I am in a tailspin. Things are really quiet and slow.

My husband's cousin said he knew a magician who worked all the time. He wasn't the best and knew it, but he was a hustler, going after jobs with incredible confidence! This magician said he used to see other magicians practicing and practicing at the magic shop but never working.

Here's the question . . . Were these hard working magicians using the practicing as procrastination to avoid doing the tough work it takes to get jobs, having a lack of confidence, needing to get better at their craft or just not knowing what to do to move forward and so kept practicing?

Probably all of the above.

Amelia Earhart was accused of not being the best pilot, but she not only had the best publicist in town in her husband GP, she was also fearless, competitive, passionate and filled with the ultimate drive in her desire to do whatever she wanted in order to accomplish her dreams and let nothing stand in her way.

Maybe that is what killed her in the end, but throughout her life, the joy she felt in just doing was palpable, "The best way to do it, is to do it!" Not waiting around for things to be done took her to great "heights" in going after and accomplishing what others attempted, tried, may have done in part, or just wanted to do. "Never interrupt someone doing something you said couldn't be done." I must do the same. As my career coach Dallas Travers says, "Don't wait to be perfect, just do it. Perfectionism is a form of procrastination."

Today is the first day of jumping in, not waiting for someone else to help me or give me the magic key to unlock my future.

I must go for the gold, but step by step, not getting overwhelmed.

Come along. Go for your "Gold."

Chapter Ten

LAST FLIGHT

ANALYSIS OF LACK OF FOCUS:

Too Many Irons In The Fire Contributed To Her Demise On Last Flight.
Written September 10, 2011

Some of the criticism of Amelia's last flight was centered around the idea that she took on too much: she was a promoter, flier, lecturer, manager of family affairs and supervisor of construction of the house in Toluca Lake, California. In the midst of all this, she even found herself giving last minute notes for the 99s newsletter.

This occurred to me this morning as I am preparing for my performance of my one-woman show, *Amelia Earhart: In Her Own Words*.

I am also focusing on getting my film and television career up to another level. I have not been passionate about my career in a long time. It feels good to be driven again. I feel better than I have felt since or even before my car accident with my mother, which devolved into a downward spiral for her and for me. My placement of Mother into a convalescent home, my personal conflict on how best to care for her, and ultimately, dealing with her death over these past two years have consumed all my mental energy and deflected my focus away from acting (at the time of this entry).

Lately though, I have missed the drive, excitement, passion, goal reaching and am deliriously joyful to be getting it back.

With that said, it occurred to me that I may not be concentrating enough on the rehearsal of my show. I have people coming that have heard about it for many years. I need to excel – and I will.

Like Amelia, I am a multitasker. I think most women are – or is that sexist?

I feel good doing many things and getting them all done. The trick is to do them all equally well, set priorities and not overlook details.

In Amelia's case, did she overlook details that ultimately caused her demise, or was she like me right now? Did she feel confident knowing she had done endurance flights before and was capable of, as she would say, "Getting the job done"? I must ponder these questions.

Each time I have performed my show, at different times in my life, I have gained a new perspective about Amelia – and about myself as well. At this moment, I am really searching to determine whether the criticism – viz. that taking on too much responsibility results in failure – is valid for both of us.

Amelia, throughout her life was not just *attempting* to do many things at once; she did them – successfully, whole-heartedly, and confidently.

Dear Reader . . .

Where do you stand on this issue? Are you a multitasker, or do you like to focus 100% on one important item at a time?

Do you think that it is possible or impossible to do a task well if you are doing many things at once?

What is your take so far on our friend Amelia?

ANALYSIS OF LACK OF FOCUS (CONTINUED)

Letters sent to Amelia's mother from Ognotz School – if we can believe that she was not just making them up to keep her mom happy – show that even as a schoolgirl, she enjoyed the balancing act of many activities. I seem to also.

From reading her personal notes and letters, and observing how she conducted her life decision-wise, I can see that the "last flight" was in keeping with the manner of her lifestyle.

Make a decision, then don't question it – just go for it. Amelia's daring since childhood exemplifies this lifelong trait; some would call it decisiveness, others might see it as careless disregard. But in any case, she was bold, fearless and resolute once she made up her mind.

I imagine when Amelia informed her parents she would like to learn to fly, they rolled their eyes and thought: "Here we go again with our Meile."

A "tomboy" by her own admission, she sought out adventure, speed, and breaking barriers. To this end she kept a scrapbook of news articles about women entering professions formerly closed to them: female fire fighters, directors, politicians, etc.

This probably endeared and connected her with independent women of like mind, such as Eleanor Roosevelt, who spoke out and followed the path they deemed right for themselves, whether it conformed to gender expectations or not.

Also, there was the momentum of women's rights and self-determination in America. The Twenty-first Amendment had recently been adopted, giving women the right to vote. It was ratified on December 5, 1933.

CONFUSION

Written March 6, 2012

Amelia's demise was attributed in large measure to poor coordination and confusing communication, both in planning and during the last leg of her round-the-world flight.

In our everyday existence we encounter mixed and confusing messages all the time. Since this is usually not life threatening, we use the catch phrase "human error" or more flippantly, "just being human."

In Amelia's case, human fallibility did prove fatal. Husband GP had made plans with the US navy ship Itasca to be in the area of Howland Island to guide Earhart's Lockheed Electra to the small atoll, approximately two miles long and about a half-mile wide. Brad Washburn, who interviewed to be her navigator, said, "If you don't hit Howland, you don't hit nothin."[1]

In the case of Amelia's flight, the naval ship captain was surprised to learn late in the game that he was to meet Amelia's plane. The Itasca did arrive in the vicinity of Howland Island and was positioned to guide the Lockheed Electra. However, the radio communication was completely misinterpreted. Amelia was listening for the Itasca on the half hour and hour. She was transmitting on the quarter hour. There seemed to be confusion as to when the Itasca was to send her messages and listen. Also, the Itasca crew could hear her, but she could not hear them.

The copy of the radio-transmitted communication log sadly speaks for itself:

July 2nd, at 10:22 a.m. local time Amelia and Noonan took off from Lae, New Guinea.

4:53 a.m. Earhart called the Itasca, reporting "Partly cloudy." (Howland Time: Amelia and Noonan had been flying approximately sixteen hours; having crossed the International Date Line, it is still July 2, 1937)

6:14 a.m. "Want bearing on 3105/ on hour/ Will whistle in Microphone."

7:42 a.m. The Itasca picked up the message, "We (Earhart and Noonan) must be on you, but we cannot see you but fuel is running low. Been unable to reach you by radio. We are flying at 1,000 feet."

The Itasca tried to reply, but Amelia seemed not to hear since there was no response.

7:58 a.m. Earhart: "We are circling but cannot hear you."

Itasca tried to transmit on a continuous basis and on different frequencies. But to no avail.

At 8:44 a.m. Earhart reported, "We are on the line of position 157-337 . . . We are running north and south." Nothing further was ever heard from her again.[2]

GEORGE PALMER PUTNAM Jr.

Stepson of Amelia Earhart Putnam

Above : George Putnam Jr., age 10, with stepmother Amelia Earhart.

Author Robera Bassin with George and Marie Palmer Putnam, Jr. 2008.

George Putnam Jr., Amelia's stepson, has watched with amusement all the efforts to find Amelia Earhart over the years. He believed the plane Earhart was flying ran out of gas and was lost at sea.

George Putnam Jr., 90 at the time of this entry, was less mobile with age and hard of hearing, but he still had clear memories of his stepmother, Amelia Earhart.

At nine, his mother brought him to Florida to help treat his polio; he never left. He was sixteen when Amelia disappeared. He watched his father, famed publisher George P. Putnam, spend time and money in a search that went nowhere.

Whenever a famous person dies in a mysterious way, speculation thrives. The greater the legend, the greater the volume of theories and range of plausibility.

George Putnam Jr. had heard it all. Some thought Earhart and Noonan ran off together, or that she was Tokyo Rose, the radio propaganda queen. Many believed she returned to America under an assumed name, to live out her life as an anonymous homemaker. People claiming to be her descendants have approached the Putnams. Others claim to have seen the couple in Saipan, imprisoned and shot by Japanese soldiers as spies. The list of theories and questionable "sightings" is innumerable.

A breakfast for George Palmer Putnam Jr. and his wife Marie was held on the morning of April 5, 2008. I had the honor of performing my one-woman show for George Putnam Jr. and his aviation friends.

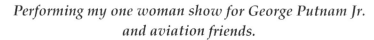

Performing my one woman show for George Putnam Jr. and aviation friends.

STANDING *(Left to Right)* George W. Crabtree, Daniel Witkoff, Bob Vanderveen, Gene Tissot Jr., Elgen Long, John Underwood, Ned Bassin
SEATED *(Left to Right)* Rhonda Towne, Roberta Bassin, Kay Otto Long, Mary Underwood, Jonna Doolittle Hoppes, Norma Tissot, Heather Gamble, and Giacinta Bradley Koontz
FRONT Marie and George Putnum, Jr.

The USNS Amelia Earhart Launched April 6, 2008
NASSCO Shipyard, San Diego, California

The author, Roberta Bassin with Marie and George Palmer Putnam Jr.

George Jr. and his wife Marie, upon seeing my show *Amelia Earhart: In Her Own Words*, commented:

"You can see your heart is in it. Amelia Earhart is a part of you."

It was truly a highlight of my career. I had always wondered if the Junior Mr. Putnam would like, approve of and enjoy my performance in the role of his stepmother, Amelia Earhart. To my joy and satisfaction, HE DID!!!

I still hold my breath at the thought of earning his approval, which meant so much to me. Thank you, George and Marie Putnam. The next day, the Putnams and all the aviation event goers attended the launching of the USNS Amelia Earhart Naval vessel to great fanfare. It was a weekend to remember.

ALCOHOLISM

Did Amelia drink alcohol, socially or otherwise?
Written July 7, 2013

I have never read of Amelia drinking any alcohol anywhere, at any time. Indeed, she was not naive about alcohol and its effects. As a girl, Amelia saw her father go from a warm, playful father to an angry alcoholic in a very short period of time. He did finally conquer the addiction late in his life.

Moreover, in the world of aviation, many pilots drank to pass the time waiting for good weather to fly their planes. Wilmer Stultz, Captain of the Friendship, on which Amelia became the first female to cross the Atlantic, was inebriated most of the time while waiting out the thirteen days for good weather to take off from Newfoundland. Amelia finally said, "We are taking off irregardless [sic] of whether Stultz is sober or not."

Of course, the most renowned incident is Amelia's last flight. Fred Noonan, her navigator on her round-the-world flight, was known as the best in his field. He was also known to be a hard drinker.

On Amelia's last phone call from Lae, New Guinea to GP (as mentioned in chapter seven), she was encouraged to discontinue the flight due to Fred Noonan's drinking. Perhaps she felt so close to completion, perhaps she can be accused of being a pathological optimist, or perhaps she simply felt familiar with how to deal with alcoholic men, predominately her father, throughout her life. Whatever the reason, Amelia made the final – and what proved to be deadly – decision to continue taking off on July 2, 1937 from Lae, New Guinea toward completion of her round-the-world flight.

Her disappearance over the Pacific, never arriving at Howland Island, caused the largest search for a private aircraft in modern history. To this day, no trace of Amelia Earhart or her navigator Fred Noonan has ever been found.

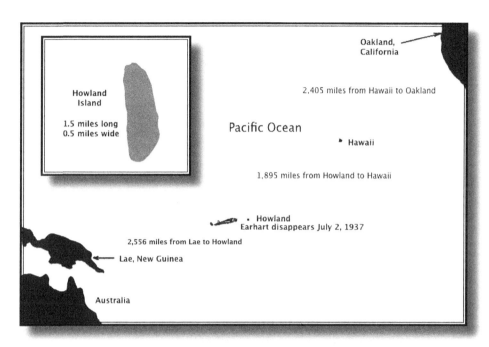

Howland
Island

1.5 miles long
0.5 miles wide

Oakland,
California

2,405 miles from Hawaii to Oakland

Pacific Ocean

• Hawaii

1,895 miles from Howland to Hawaii

• Howland
Earhart disappears July 2, 1937

2,556 miles from Lae to Howland

Lae, New Guinea

Australia

Earhart and Noonan departed from Lae, Papua New Guinea, for the longest stretch. Their destination was Howland Island, a tiny (1.5 mile by 1/2 mile-wide or 2.4 by 0.8 kilometer) atoll rising a mere 20 feet (6 meters) from the Pacific.

Did alcohol play a part in the fatal flight? There is no way to determine the answer definitively. There were many factors at play: Her plane ran out of fuel, her maps of Howland Island were off by five miles, she had been flying for twenty-three hours, which causes, as she herself had once noted, "seeing territory that should be annexed by the USA" in the water's shadows, an effect of exhaustion. This, coupled with the rising sun in her eyes, not knowing how to use her radio or Morse code to communicate properly with the ship Itasca (which should have guided her to Howland) along with husband George's lack of knowledge in setting up that very plan with the navy, was a recipe for disaster.

Amelia is a legend, a mystery, an inspiration, a very private, yet the ultimate public figure, who broke barriers, spoke her mind, followed her passion, and as Hillary Clinton said, "Is still an inspiration making us think bigger and broader."[3]

Amelia's husband George put pressure on the government, writing to Sumner Wells of the US State Department requesting an additional search of a specific position at once in a letter dated August 4, 1937. The official search lasted two weeks, officially ending July18th after Amelia's disappearance on July 2, 1937.

> Dear Mr. Wells,
> I deeply appreciate your friendly cooperation. I will be further grateful if it be possible for you to follow up this matter now that search of the position given may be undertaken at once. It is of course a forlorn hope, but one which, you will understand, is of the upmost concern to me.
>
> Please spare no effort in bringing it about if you possibly can,
> > Sincerely,
> > GPP[4]

It breaks one's heart, as George and the nation feared the worst.

Dear Reader . . .

What are your thoughts about Amelia's decisiveness to continue from Lae, New Guinea on her round-the-world last flight?

Was Amelia just being a confident flier?

Was it the idea that once she set a goal, it must be completed?

Was she being illogical?

Plenty of room for a discussion.

Her husband George continued the search for Amelia long after the government terminated the official search. Is there any question in your mind that George loved his Amelia?

What is your view?

"FLYING AS COMMONPLACE"

Written August 10, 2013

"I predict that commercial flying will be as normal as train travel is today," predicted Amelia. She used her celebrity "to promote flying as common place."[5]

I sit outside at 9:17 p.m. on a clear summer night with a touch of coolness, so pleasant, looking up at the cloudless sky and identifying some of the constellations.

But wait, one, and then another of the stars is moving and flashing so high in the sky.

Is it a bird? Is it a plane? Is it Superman? No, No, No! It is beyond the speed of a plane. It is the age of fast jets, space station and helicopters, proving our heroine was right. Flying IS "as commonplace as train travel" or any form of travel was once.

Tonight, I enjoy determining if I am seeing a distant twinkling star, a fast moving jet or the space station circumnavigating the globe every ninety-two minutes. Thanks to incredible technology, NASA will notify the average citizen (like my husband) by email when the space station is visible in our area!

NEW FANGLED TECHNOLOGY
JUST CHANGE OR PROGRESS?

Written January 24, 2012

Amelia never learned Morse code or how to properly use radio equipment.

Can we really fault her? I say this with sympathy after trying to learn how to navigate the high-speed technological changes in our everyday environment. The frustration of trying to pay for parking now with automated meters, learning to download – or is it upload? – a movie, or just trying to delete incorrect information once it is on the Internet. ACHHHHHHHH! I could (and sometimes do) just scream with frustration throwing my hands up, and yet trying the next day once again, for change (or progress whichever your point of view), is inevitable.

Amelia's round-the-world flight was to be her last. "I plan to give up long distance stunt flying," she said. "It's hard to grow old, so hard. I think, GP that I shall not live to grow old."[6]

Maybe, even at thirty-nine, almost forty, change and challenge were taking their toll on America's most famous and the world's most renowned female of the 20th century.

Dear Reader . . .

How do you feel about new technology?

Does it frustrate you, are you adapting, or do you welcome it?

Or is it all of the above?

THE NEW TECHNOLOGY
"MORE" NEW TECHNOLOGY

Written September 15, 2011

I'm sitting outside by my pool (very Californian) and I am playing with my latest computer-type toy, the iPad, which is supposed to make day-to-day life even faster, more improved than last week's technology.

I fought the computer age tooth and nail, avoiding it when possible. But like a tidal wave, things keep moving. Businesses start to utilize the new tools, adults buy them, bring them home, the kids pick them up. It's their new world, well, it is their only world. It becomes our new world. So here I am finding the advantages and disadvantages of the brave new faster-than-light-speed everyday use of my iPad.

In fact, in the last three days, I've started to use my iPhone, iMac and iPad all lined up together – cutting, pasting, utilizing all three as one unit!!!!!!

Again I am reminded of Amelia's dislike or avoidance of using modern radio equipment and lack of knowledge of technology and radio communications on her final flight, which most experts agree could have saved her and Noonan.

GP has been blamed, for he had little knowledge of aircraft but was left in charge due to the resignation of technical expert Paul Mantz and expert radioman Harry Manning. Thus, expert guidance was limited.

Brad Washburn had ". . . told them they needed to set up radio communications systems on Howland Island. If not that, then to carry special low frequency radio equipment. That would enable ships to locate her." [Amelia] asked GP "What do you think?" GP felt there was not enough time if they wanted to be back by July 4th. "If you go to all that trouble, the book will not be out for the Christmas sales."[7]

218

Brad Washburn
(June 7,1910 -Jan.10,2007)
Famous navigator, adventurer
and explorer interviewed to be the
navigator for Amelia's round-the-
world flight.

Amelia never needed the new technology and had done fine before. As Brad Washburn said, "Europe, you can't miss it. But there is something very lonely about that Pacific."[8]

According to Gore Vidal (Gene Vidal's son), Amelia's biggest fear was flying over Africa. She felt if she went down there, they would never find her. "What about the Pacific? That's very big," questioned Gore. She confidently responded, "Oh you can't miss an island."[9]

My mother said she never thought she would not change with the times. For example, when cars entered the scene, people would yell, "Get a horse!" After all, it got you there, and didn't break down as quickly. But young people accept the new and the different as they separate themselves from their elders. We either learn or are left behind. Amelia could not adjust to the new technology. She had managed to successfully conquer oceans and continents without the aid of radio or Morse code. Maybe that is why, in part, she said, "It is hard to grow old, so hard." We like to work with what we learned and used growing up. Change, learning anew and putting that into practice can be daunting and uncomfortable

Now the mystery continues: movies, books, documentaries, private researchers . . . all searching for the lost heroine of the skies along with Fred Noonan, the navigator of the Lockheed Electra. Supposition as to what happened and why has turned a legend in her own time into a legend for all times.

EPILOGUE

A personal confession
A note of encouragement to my readers:

I found that each time I edited my pages for "Amelia Earhart, Me and Our Friends," I found encouragement through Amelia's words. It kept me going on the book and gave me solace in tough times, smiles in happy times, and food for thought when I was pensive.

I also found that the personal memories and thoughts which I shared with you, dear readers "our friends," gave me that "Oh Yes, I remember it well" to coin a Maurice Chevalier song.

I am so surprised how my little book has and continues to help me navigate life's ups and downs.

My hope is that Amelia will or has helped you as you have read, written, shared and remembered along with us, to work out some of your "ups and downs" as we take the journey that, as my dear Aunt Lillian would say, "That's Life."

I wrote this book because I had a nagging need to take my knowledge of Amelia Earhart and my personal journey connected with her as a performer and researcher and put it into a book.

Why have I done this book?

In part, to prove to myself that I could write and publish a book, almost embarrassed if anyone might read it, equally scared to have a family member or friend pre-read it, or ask a notable friend to write a "Foreword." That is the hardest part for me and I am learning from other writers as well. Thank you to my friend, Giacinta Bradley Koontz for sharing her fears as a writer and all the support and help she has given me along the way.

As Amelia put it . . .

To want in one's heart to do a thing, for its own sake; to enjoy doing it; to concentrate all one's energies upon it – that is not only the surest guarantee of its success, it is also being true to oneself. If there is anything I have learned in life it is this: If you follow the inner desire of your heart, the incidentals will take care of themselves.

REFERENCES AND SOURCES

UNPUBLISHED
Bassin, Roberta E.
 Amelia Earhart: In Her Own Words Copyright: Library of Congress.

(The following references were used in writing the play *Amelia Earhart: In Her Own Words*. Thus they are included by osmosis in this book, *Amelia Earhart, Me and Our Friends*.)

PUBLISHED BOOKS
Backus, Jean L.
 Letters from Amelia. Beacon Press 1982

Earhart, Amelia.
 AMELIA EARHART Last Flight. Harcourt, Brace, and World, 1937.
 20 Hrs. 40 Min. New York: G. P. Putnam's Sons, 1928.
 The Fun of It. New York: Harcourt, Brace, and World 1932, 1987.

Knootnz, Giacinta Bradley.
 Harriet Quimby Scrapbook: The Life of America's First Birdwoman.
 Running Iron Publications, 2003.

Long, Elgen M. and Mary K.
 Amelia Earhart: The Mystery Solved. A Touchstone Book published by
 Simon & Schuster, 1999.

Lovell, Mary S.
 The Sound of Wings, The Life of Amelia Earhart. New York, N.Y. : St.
 Martin's Press.

Morrissey, Muriel Earhart.
 Courage is the Price. Wichita, Kansas: Wichita, Kansas: McCormick-
 Armstrong Publishing Division, 1963.
 My Courageous Sister. Santa Clara, California: Osborn Publishing,
 1987

Randolph, Blythe.
  Amelia Earhart. New York, London/ Toronto/ Sydney: Franklin, Watts.

Rich, Doris.
  Amelia Earhart A Biography. Washington & London: Smithsonian
  Institution Press.

NEWSPAPERS IDENTIFIED
Los Angeles Times June 21, 2001 by Phil McCombs Washington Post
Los Angeles Times April 22, 2001 by Cecilia Rasmussen

DOCUMENTARY
PBS: *The Price of Courage*

PHOTO CREDITS

WIth appreciation to all those who provided photographs, paintings and drawings, many of which although not included, were warmly received giving permission for their use. All manner of research and effort to locate the original sources has been put forth. Any omission is regrettably unavoidable.

Pictures not credited are in my private collections.

COVER

Right: Author, Roberta Ellen Bassin. Photo: Ned Franklin Bassin at The Santa Monica Museum of Flying. Author's Personal Collection.

Left: One of a series of publicity shots of Amelia Earhart, taken on the roof of the Copley Plaza in Boston prior to the 1928 transatlantic flight. Courtesy Smithsonian National Air and Space Museum (NASM 78-16945), Mary E. "Mother" Tusch Collection. (http://siarchives.si.edu).

CHAPTER ONE

p. 1 [Title Page] Amelia Earhart writing in front of a fireplace: Courtesy of Purdue University Libraries, Karnes Archives and Special Collections.

p. 10 Amelia Earhart, 1903 age six. Courtesy of The Schlesinger Library, Radcliffe Institute, Harvard University.

p. 11 Amelia Earhart with her mother, Amy Otis Earhart. May, 1933. Courtesy of The Schlesinger Library on the History of Women in America, Radcliffe Institute.

CHAPTER TWO

p. 19 [Title Page] Amelia Earhart poses with an unidentified man during her lecture tour following the Friendship flight of 1928. Photo: Courtesy Cradle of Aviation Museum, NY.

p. 23 Author Roberta Bassin taken at Clay Lacy's Aviation. Photo: Ned Franklin Bassin; Author's Personal Collection.

p. 27 [Left] Hands of Amelia Earhart: Courtesy of Purdue University Libraries, Karnes Archives and Special Collections.

p. 27 [Right] George Palmer Putnam and Amelia Earhart hands on world globe ca. 1937: Courtesy of Purdue University Libraries, Karnes Archives and Special Collections.

p. 31 [Top] Dress designed by Amelia Earhart taken at Amelia Earhart's Birthplace Museum in Atchison Kansas: Author's Personal Collection.

p. 31 [Bottom] Author with Amelia Earhart Luggage taken at Amelia Earhart's Birthplace Museum in Atchison Kansas: Author's Personal Collection.

p. 34 Harriet Quimby (1875-1912) Flying costume worn for Cross-Channel Flight 1912; [Inset] US postage stamp issued in 1991. Images: *The Harriet Quimby Scrapbook, the Life of America's first Birdwoman* by Giacinta Bradley Koontz.

p. 35 Amelia Earhart in Jodhpurs. Courtesy of OAC (Online Archive of California) Kern County Library.

CHAPTER THREE

p. 37 [Title Page] L to R: Amelia Earhart, Noretah Holmes, Frances Marsalis, and Betty Huyler Gillies. Taken at a Ninety-Nines roller-skating party, Roosevelt Field, Long Island, NY, ca. 1930s. Photo: Courtesy Cradle of Aviation Museum, NY.

p. 38 Roberta E. Bassin posing with a statue of Amelia Earhart at the Forest of Friendship near Atchison, Kansas. Photo: Giacinta Bradley Koontz; Author's Personal Collection.

p. 39 L to R: Rhonda Towne, Roberta Bassin, Giacinta Bradley Koontz in Atchison, Kansas while attending the Amelia Earhart Festival July 2009: Author's Personal Collection.

p. 43 [Left] Amy Otis Earhart holding her infant daughter, Amelia Earhart. Photo: Courtesy Elgen M. Long Collection.

p. 43 [Right] Sally Kaufman hugs her young daughter, Roberta E. Bassin. Photo: Author's Personal Collection.

CHAPTER FOUR

p. 67 [Title Page] Amelia Earhart waves to the crowd at Southhampton, England, following her flight across the Atlantic Ocean as a passenger on the Friendship flight in 1928. Photo: Courtesy Cradle of Aviation Museum, NY.

p. 69 [Top] Crashed Lockheed Electra (10E) with Amelia Earhart standing on wing, takeoff from Hawaii on first attempt for her round-the-world flight March 1937 Further reference: "A Round-the-World Flight Ends in the Pacific," and "Log of Earhart's Last Stunt Flight," *Life* Magazine, July 19, 1937, Volume 3, Number 3.

p. 69 [Bottom] Amelia Earhart ground looped on takeoff at Luke Field, Hawaii, March 20, 1937, damaging the tire and making it unable to fly. The damaged propellers and engine cowlings have already been removed. The fuselage fuel tanks are being emptied. Amelia Earhart in Hawaii images used with permission from Matson Archives.

CHAPTER FIVE

p. 81 [Title Page] Amelia Earhart and George Palmer Putnam walking hand-in-hand at the Oakland, California Airport, ca. 1930s. Photo: Courtesy Smithsonian National Air and Space Museum (#NASM 82-8669).

p. 82 [Top] Wedding photo of author Roberta and Ned Bassin. Author's Personal Collection.

p. 82 [Bottom] Oil portrait of Amelia and George Palmer Putnam's 1931 wedding photo; hangs in the Amelia Earhart Birthplace Museum, Atchison, Kansas. Photo: Courtesy Giacinta Bradley Koontz.

p. 83 Amelia Earhart's pre-nuptial letter to George Palmer Putnam. Courtesy Purdue University Libraries, Karnes Archives and Special Collections.

p. 93 [Top] Amelia Earhart and her husband George Palmer Putnam, at the Hotel Lotti, Paris, France, following her solo flight across the Atlantic Ocean in 1932. Photo: Courtesy Purdue University Libraries, Karnes Archives and Special Collections.

p. 93 [Bottom] Husband Ned Franklin Bassin and author Roberta E. Bassin. Living Legends of Aviation Gala at The Beverly Hilton Hotel, California. Author's Personal Collection.

CHAPTER SIX

p. 105 [Title Page] Amelia Earhart on Horseback. Photo: Courtesy Purdue University Libraries, Karnes Archives and Special Collections.

p. 108 Muriel and Amelia Earhart playing, 1906. Courtesy of The Schlesinger Library, Radcliffe Institute, Harvard University.

p. 113 Amelia Earhart modeling a dress from her fashion design collection. Insert: Clothing label for *Amelia Earhart Clothing Designs*. Images: Courtesy Purdue University Libraries, Karnes Archives and Special Collections.

p. 119 Roberta E. Bassin at age five in her first year at ballet school taught by Jan Robinson in Beverly Hills in the Wilshire District, California. Author's Personal Collection.

p. 122 Amelia Earhart just in from the surf on Waikiki Beach, Oahu, Hawaii, ca. 1935. Amelia Earhart in Hawaii images used with permission from Matson Archives.

p. 123 Amelia and George being serenaded by musicians, ca. 1935 Amelia Earhart in Hawaii images used with permission from Matson Archives.

p. 124 Amelia Earhart's copper watering can. Courtesy Elgen M. Long Collection.

p. 130 Amelia, Muriel, their father, Edwin and the porter, Tomiko, on the end of a railroad car. Courtesy of The Schlesinger Library, Radcliffe Institute.

CHAPTER SEVEN

p. 133 [Title Page] Amelia Earhart poses in front of her Lockheed Electra (date and place unknown). Photo: Courtesy Cradle of Aviation Museum, NY.

p. 139 Amelia Earhart's red Lockheed Vega 5B (NR-7952) displayed at the Smithsonian National Air and Space Museum, Washington, D.C. Photo: Author's Personal Collection.

p. 140 [Top] Roberta Bassin at Smithsonian National Air and Space Museum. Author's Personal Collection.

p. 140 [Bottom] Amelia Earhart stands in front of her Lockheed Electra 10E. Photo: The John Underwood Collection.

p. 144 L to R: Amy Guest, Lou Gordon, Amelia Earhart, Wilmer Stultz, Mrs. Foster Welch. Southampton, England 1928. Photo: Courtesy Purdue University Libraries, Karnes Archives and Special Collections.

CHAPTER EIGHT

p. 155 [Title Page] Amelia Earhart waves to the crowds during the New York City ticker-tape parade honoring her solo flight across the Atlantic Ocean in 1932. Photo: Courtesy Cradle of Aviation Museum, NY.

p. 164 Roberta E. Bassin in front of the Amelia Earhart Birthplace Museum, Atchison, Kansas. Photo: Author's Personal Collection.

CHAPTER NINE

p. 171 [Title Page] Photo taken in 1937 for Amelia Earhart's *World Flight (A Woman's Achievement) Book*, that was to be written upon her return. Photograph from the Albert Bresnick Collection; Courtesy Giacinta Bradley Koontz.

p. 180 Amelia Earhart and First Lady Eleanor Roosevelt, 1933. Photo: Courtesy Purdue University Libraries, Karnes Archives and Special Collections.

CHAPTER TEN

p. 197 [Title Page] Amelia Earhart's flight crew and advisors for her first attempt to circumnavigate the globe in 1937 included: L to R: Paul Mantz, Amelia Earhart, Harry Manning, and Fred Noonan. Photo: Courtesy Purdue University Libraries, Karnes Archives and Special Collections.

p. 205 Left: George Palmer Putnam, Jr. age ten, with his step-mother, Amelia Earhart, ca. 1931. *Palm Beach Post*, Obituary for Putnam dated September 1, 2013.

p. 205 Right: George Putnam, Jr., Roberta E. Bassin and his wife Marie at breakfast honoring the Putnams, San Diego, California. Photo: Ned Franklin Bassin; Author's Personal Collection.

p. 206 Attendees at the breakfast honoring George and Marie Putnam on the occasion of the launch of the *USNS Amelia Earhart (T-AKE 6)*, San Diego, California. Photo: Author's Personal Collection.

p. 207 Roberta E. Bassin with Marie and George Putnam at the launch of the US Navy's supply ship, *USNS Amelia Earhart (T-AKE 6)*, April 6, 2008. Photo: Ned Franklin Bassin; Author's Personal Collection.

p. 209 Inset: Map of Howland Island. Designed by Ned Franklin Bassin

p. 209 Map of Howland Island in relationship to; Aisa, Australia, Lei, New Guinea, Hawaii and West Coast of the USA. Designed by Ned Franklin Bassin.

p. 219 Left: Henry Bradford "Brad" Washburn, at the Boston Museum of Science. Right: A youthful Washburn ready to photograph mountains in Alaska, ca. 1941. Photos: Courtesy of the Boston Museum of Science.

p. 220 Amelia Earhart and her navigator Fred Noonan en route on their round-the-world flight, 1937. Photo: Courtesy Special Collections Department-McDermott Library, History of Aviation Collection, Special Collections and Archives Division, Eugene McDermott Library, The University of Texas at Dallas.

BACK COVER

Head Shot of Roberta E. Bassin: Author's Personal Collection.

Amelia Earhart wearing a matching plaid skirt, sweater and coat, stands in front of her Lockheed Vega. Photo: Courtesy of the 99s Museum of Women Pilots, Oklahoma, and Giacinta Bradley Koontz.

FOOTNOTES

INTRODUCTION:
1. Footnote: Hillary Clinton's Speech (March 20, 2012 U.S. Department of State. Remarks at an event Celebrating Amelia Earhart & The United States' Ties to Our Pacific Neighbors) http://www.state.gov/secretary/20092013clinton/rm/2012/03/186072.htm

Chapter 1: WE WRITE, RIGHT.
1. *Amelia Earhart* by Doris L. Rich p. 11
2. *The Fun of It* by Amelia Earhart p. 20
3. *Letters from Amelia* by Jean L. Backus p. 9
4. *Amelia Earhart: In Her Own Words* by Roberta Bassin
5. Letters from Amelia by Jean L Backus p. 198-199
6. *Last Flight* by Amelia Earhart p. 60
7. *Last Flight* by Amelia Earhart p. 41
8. Itasca Log also in *The Sound of Wings* by Mary S. Lovell p. 341

Chapter 2: FASHION, FUN and PHYSICAL APPEARANCE
1. *Amelia Earhart: In Her Own Words* by Roberta Bassin
2. *Amelia Earhart: In Her Own Words* by Roberta Bassin
3. Lockheed Electra parts vocabulary: http://divegame.net/node/107462 (steer wheel)
4. *Letters from Amelia* by Jean L. Backus p. 199
5. *Pilot in Pearls* by Shirley Dobson Gilroy p. 56
   Living the Dream . . . Amelia's statement from Internet article *Secrets of Success*

Chapter 3: FAMILY and FRIENDS
1. Cousin Nancy Morse interview *The Price of Courage* PBS documentary
2. *Amelia Earhart* by Blythe Randolph p. 97
3. *Letters from Amelia* by Jean L. Backus p. 78
4. *Letters from Amelia* by Jean L. Backus p. 80
5. *Letters from Amelia* by Jean L. Backus p. 29
   The word "bought" is written "bot" by Amelia.

6. *Letters from Amelia* by Jean L. Backus p. 119
   1931 letter (Letters from Amelia: p. 119 by Jean Backus. The word, "you" is "yu" written by Amelia.
7. *Letters from Amelia* by Jean L. Backus p. 176
8. *Letters from Amelia* by Jean L. Backus p. 144
9. *Letters from Amelia* by Jean L. Backus p. 137
10. *Amelia Earhart: In Her Own Words* by Roberta Bassin.

Chapter 4: WEAK CONSTITUTION, STRONG DETERMINATION
1. *Last Flight* by Amelia Earhart p. 39
2. *The Price of Courage* PBS Documentary
3. *Realizing the Dream of Flight* edited by Virginia p Dawson and Mark D. Bowles p. 36
4. *Last Flight* by Amelia Earhart p. 60
5. Gore Vidal interview: *The Price of Courage* PBS Documentary
6. *Last Flight* by Amelia Earhart p. 8
7. Amelia Earhart. (n.d.). BrainyQuote.com. Retrieved January 14, 2016, from BrainyQuote.com Web site: http://www.brainyquote.com/quotes/quotes/a/ameliaearh403311.html
8. *20 Hrs. 40 Min.* by Amelia Earhart p.V intro by Marion Perkins
9. *20 Hrs. 40 Min.* by Amelia Earhart p. 70 (1928 version) also in *Amelia Earhart: The Turbulent Life of an Ameican Icon* p.41

Chapter 5: THE RELATIONSHIP
1. *Letters From Amelia* by Jean L. Backus
2. Marriage Letter (uneditied): *The Sound of Wings* by Mary S. Lovell
3. *Letters From Amelia* by Jean L. Backus p. 107
4. Sally Chapman's interview: *The Price of Courage* PBS Documentary
5. *Letters From Amelia* p. 69, and *Amelia Earhart in Her Own Words* by Robert Bassin, Courtesy of Purdue University Libraries, Karnes Archives and Special Collections.
6. *Amelia Earhart* by Blythe Randolph p. 53
7. *Amelia Earhart* by Blythe Randolph p. 39
8. *Amelia Earhart* by Blythe Randolph p. 69
9. *The Fun of It* by Amelia Earhart p. 98
10. *The Price of Courage* PBS Documentary
11. *Los Angeles Times* 6/12/2001 by Phil McCombs
12. *Letters From Amelia* by Jean L.Backus p. 139
13. *Last Flight* by Amelia Earhart p. 14

14. Purdue University Archives Research: GP Letter to Nilla, Courtesy of Purdue University Libraries, Karnes Archives and special Collections.

Chapter 6: ACTIVITIES-NOT JUST A FLIER BY ANY MEANS
1. *The Fun Of It* by Amelia Earhart p. 8
2. *The Fun Of It* by Amelia Earhart p. 9
3. *Amelia Earhart: In Her Own Words* by Roberta Bassin
4. *The Fun Of It* by Amelia Earhart p. 12
5. *The Fun Of It* by Amelia Earhart p. 11
6. *The Fun Of It* by Amelia Earhart p. 12
7. *The Fun Of It* by Amelia Earhart p. 18
8. *Amelia Earhart: In Her Own Words* by Roberta Bassin
9. *Amelia Earhart* by Blythe Randolf p. 17
10. *One Day In May* by Joe Campbell (internet).
11. *Last Flight* by Amelia Earhart p. 15
12. *Courage is the Price* by Muriel Earhart Morrissey p. 73

Chapter 7: PERSPECTIVES and FLIGHT
1. *Amelia Earhart* by Blythe Randolph p. 65-66
2. *Last Flight* by Amelia Earhart p. 46
3. *Amelia Earhart* by Doris L. Rich p. 19
4. Amelia's Prenuptial letter to George Palmer Putnam; Courtesy of Purdue University Libraries, Karnes Archives and Special Collections.
5. *The Price of Courage* PBS Documentary

Chapter 8: PERSONALITY
1. *Last Flight* by Amelia Earhart p. XVI
2. *Last Flight* by Amelia Earhart Introduction p. XVi
3. Famous quotations (Internet Stratus Project)
4. *Letters From Amelia* by Jean L. Backus p. 137
5. *Letters From Amelia* by Jean L. Backus p. 119
6. *Amelia Earhart: In Her Own Words* by Roberta Bassin
7. *Letters From Amelia* by Jean L. Backus p. 27
8. *Amelia Earhart* by Blythe Randolph p. 69
9. *Amelia Earhart: In Her Own Words* by Roberta Bassin

Chapter 9: GOALS

1. *The Fun of It* by Amelia Earhart p. 25
2. *The Price of Courage* PBS Documentary
3. *Last Flight* by Amelia Earhart p. 60
4. *Last Flight* by Amelia Earhart p. 133
5. *Last Flight* by Amelia Earhart p. xvii

Chapter 10: LAST FLIGHT
1. Brad Washburn, *The Price of Courage* PBS Documentary
2. Communications Log: 7:42 a.m. Doris Rich p. 268-269
   Communications Log: *The Sound of Wings*, Mary S. Lovell p. 336-341
3. Hillary Clinton Speech, March 20, 2012 U.S. Department of State.
4. Purdue Archives
5. *Amelia Earhart: In Her Own Words* by Roberta Bassin
6. *Amelia Earhart: In Her Own Words* by Roberta Bassin
7. *Los Angeles Times* June 12, 2001
8. *The Price of Courage* PBS Documentary
9. *The Price of Courage* PBS Documentary

AMELIA EARHART:
A TIMELINE OF LIFE EVENTS

❖ 1897 Born in Atchison, Kansas on July 24th, Amelia Mary Earhart, to Edwin and Amy Otis Earhart.

❖ 1900 Amelia's sister, Muriel, born in Kansas City, Kansas.

❖ 1904 Amelia helps build and slides down backyard roller coaster.

❖ 1907 Parents Edwin and Amy Otis Earhart move to Des Moines, Iowa. Girls stay with grandparents for a year, then follow.

❖ 1908 Amelia sees first airplane at Iowa State Fair in Des Moines.

❖ 1910 Father, Edwin Earhart, becomes an alcoholic. Difficult times for the family.

❖ 1913 Family moves to St. Paul, Minnesota.

❖ 1916 Amelia Graduates from Hyde Park High in Chicago, Illinois, which she chose for its chemistry laboratory.

❖ 1916 Fall: Enrolls in Ogontz School, junior college for women, Philadelphia, Pennsylvania.

❖ 1917 Volunteers for Red Cross service in Toronto, Canada.

❖ 1918 Sees stunt flying in Toronto, Canada.

❖ 1919 Enrolls in Columbia University, New York, as pre-med student. After one semester leaves due to family financial difficulties and to help parents in Los Angeles, California.

❖ 1919 Father is cured of alcoholism.

- ❖ 1920 Amelia takes first flight with Frank Hawks.

- ❖ 1921 Amelia makes first flight taking flying lessons from Neta Snook.

- ❖ 1921 December: Amelia receives her United States flying license.

- ❖ 1922 Amelia buys her own plane: Kinner Canary.

- ❖ 1923 May: Amelia is granted the Fédération Aéronautique Internationale flying license.

- ❖ 1922 October: Sets unofficial altitude record for women of 14,000 feet, Long Beach, California.

- ❖ 1924 Parents separate and start divorce proceedings. Amelia and mother join sister Muriel in Massachusetts.

- ❖ 1925 Hired to teach English and social work at Dennison House, Boston, Massachusetts.

- ❖ 1927 Spring: Captain H. H. Railey calls Amelia at Dennison House to consider being first woman to fly across the Atlantic. Interview follows with Publisher George Putnam, and two others in New York.

- ❖ 1928 June: Amelia flies as a passenger aboard The Friendship and becomes the first woman to cross the Atlantic Ocean by air.

- ❖ 1928 September: First woman to solo on transcontinental round trip.

- ❖ 1929 Acquires Lockheed Red Vega. Flies it in first Women's Air Derby.

- ❖ 1929 Founds the "99's:" First female pilots' organization.

- ❖ 1929 George Palmer Putnam and wife Dorothy separate.

- ❖ 1929 November: Speed record for women, Los Angeles, California.

❖ 1930 Amelia becomes First President of "99's."

❖ 1930 Amelia's father, Edwin Earhart, dies.

❖ 1930 George Palmer Putnam's divorce finalized.

❖ 1931 Amelia marries George Palmer Putnam February 7th in Noank, Connecticut.

❖ 1931 Amelia promotes autogiros: record breaking altitude of 18,415 feet at Willow Grove, Pennsylvania.

❖ 1932 May: First woman to solo across the Atlantic and first person to cross the Atlantic by air twice.

❖ 1932 Amelia awarded the National Geographic Society's Special Gold Medal, the U.S. Congressional Distinguished Flying Cross, and the French government's Cross of Knight of the Legion of Honor.

❖ 1932 August: Women's nonstop-transcontinental speed record, 19 hours 5 minutes, Los Angeles, California to Newark, New Jersey.

❖ 1933 Visits the White House and is the house guest of President and Mrs. Franklin D. Roosevelt.

❖ 1933 July: Breaks own 1931 transcontinental speed record.

❖ 1935 Makes first solo flight from Hawaii to California: First person to solo anywhere over the Pacific. First person to solo over Atlantic and Pacific oceans.

❖ 1935 May: First person to fly solo from Mexico to Newark, New Jersey.

❖ 1935 Joins faculty at Purdue University as Visiting Counselor for Women.

❖ 1936 Flies in Bendix Air Trophy Race.

* 1937 March 17th: First attempt of round-the-world-flight at the equator. Amelia Earhart and crew leave from Oakland California to Honolulu, Hawaii. Sets record for fastest crossing of 15 hours 47 minutes.

* 1937 March 20th: Second leg of first attempt round-the-world flight. Airplane, the Lockheed Electra, ground loops on take off from Honolulu, Hawaii and is severly damaged.

* 1937 May 20th: Second attempt of round-the-world flight at the equator begins. Takes off from Oakland, California Eastward to Miami, Florida in repaired Lockheed Electra.

* 1937 July 2nd: After completing approximately 24,000 miles of the 29,000 mile goal, and losing radio contact with the ship Itasca, Amelia Earhart and her navigator, Fred Noonan, disappear over the Pacific trying to reach Howland Island.